DERBYSHIRE PUBS

A Pint Sized History and Miscellany

DERBYSHIRE PUBS

PUBS

A Pint Sized History and Miscellany

MICHAEL SMITH

ACKNOWLEDGEMENTS

Several people have helped me in writing this book. I should like to express my particular thanks to the following:

Nick Smith for advice and assistance with digital photography and for providing photographs of the Quiet Woman pub.

The staff at DB Publishing for their advice, encouragement and for bringing the work to fruition.

The staffs of the following libraries, without whom the research could not have been completed:

Chesterfield Library

Derby Local Studies Library

Ilkeston Library

The Magic Attic, Swadlincote

Nottingham University Library (Hallwood and King's Meadow sites)

In completing the research for this book, I made use of a wide range of primary sources, including newspapers dating back to the 18th century. I also relied on interviews with a wide range of people. Some of the stories behind our pubs are the stuff of myth and legend and have long been acknowledged as such by historians. I have included them, however, because they remain an important element of our rich pub heritage and culture. The local pub scene is in a state of constant flux, with name changes, the closing of popular local hostelries and the opening of new micro pubs. As a consequence, no book about pubs will ever be completely up to date. Despite this, I am confident that this book will remain the definitive work on the subject for some years to come.

Michael E Smith

First Published in Great Britain in 2019 by DB Publishing,
an imprint of JMD Media Ltd

ISBN 978-1-78091-589-0

Printed and bound in the UK

CONTENTS

THE STORY OF THE DERBYSHIRE PUB

The story of Derbyshire's pubs dates back to Roman times. Taburnae, or shops that sold wine, were popular with soldiers and civilians alike, and it is likely that such places would have flourished in the settlements at Derby, Chesterfield and Buxton as well as some of the smaller civilian settlements that grew up alongside legionary forts. It seems that these taburnae quickly adapted to provide the locals with ale and the word eventually became corrupted to tavern.

The Romans also established mansiones on the sides of roads to provide food, drink and accommodation for imperial messengers and other important travellers. They served a similar function to the coaching inns of the 18th century and historians believe that some of them may have originated as privately owned inns. They generally delivered a good standard of accommodation and other services included the provision of a bath house. A number of Roman roads passed through Derbyshire, including the important Ryknild Street. It seems likely that travellers would have stayed in these mansiones as they passed through the area on important business.

By the Saxon period, wine had given way to ale, and villagers would have gathered in the local alehouse to exchange gossip, perhaps do a little business and enjoy each

The Shakespeare Inn sign.

The Quiet Woman Inn sign.

The Vernon Arms sign.   *The Bull's Head Inn sign*

other's company. By the 11th century, Derby had a population of around 700 and would probably have supported a number of these ale houses. In smaller villages the local ale house would have been little more than a simple wattle and daub structure where one of the villagers would have entertained his friends and neighbours.

By the medieval period, taverns and village ale houses in Derbyshire were often supplied with ale by the local manor house. Even at this time, however, there were commercial brewers, although their products had to be passed by an 'ale-conner' or taster before they were sold. Of course, ale continued to be brewed in the home and this task was usually undertaken by the women of the household. The widespread introduction of pub names and signs also dates from this period. From the early Middle Ages, ale stakes had been hung outside inns to indicate that ale was ready to be drunk. With the proliferation of inns and alehouses there was a need, particularly in the larger towns, to identify individual establishments; and in an age when most of the population was illiterate a simple sign was the obvious solution. Before the Reformation, many of these signs had a religious significance such as the Cross Keys, the symbol of Saint Peter. When Henry VIII made his break with the Roman Catholic Church, many landlords sought to demonstrate their loyalty to the crown by changing the name of their inn to the King's Head or the Rose and Crown.

Brewing on a larger scale was carried on in monasteries throughout Derbyshire, with the monks providing for the needs of visitors and travellers as well as their own consumption. In 1491 when John Stanley, the Abbot of Dale, was dismissed for

The Abbey pub at Darley Abbey.

'imbecility and impotence' (incompetence and lack of leadership) his pension included an allowance of eight flagons a week of the best beer. This would have been brewed in the abbey, for the inventory of 1538 mentions a brewhouse as well as a number of items used in the brewing process. The inventory of Repton Priory made in the same year (at the Dissolution of the Monasteries) lists a brewhouse, fermenting room and sifting house as well as equipment such as cauldrons, ladles and a mashing vat. It is also interesting to note that at Darley Abbey the present-day Abbey pub is believed to have been the original guest house of the abbey.

Some of the earliest inns also date from this period. Some monastic houses could not cope with the large numbers of travellers who called at their gate seeking food and shelter for the night and therefore began to establish guest houses. The Royal Oak at Chesterfield claims to have been built on the site of a

The Royal Oak
WAS BUILT IN THE 12th CENTURY
THIS IS THE OLDEST INN
IN CHESTERFIELD & ONE OF
THE OLDEST IN ENGLAND.
IT WAS FORMALLY A
REST-HOUSE FOR
"THE KNIGHTS TEMPLAR"
IN THE YEARS OF
"THE HOLY CRUSADES"
THEN THROUGH & AFTER
THE MEDIEVAL PERIOD
IT WAS USED AS TWO
BUTCHERS SHOPS
& INN ACCOMMODATION.
THE EARLIEST
DISCOVERED RECORDS
SHOW
IT ALREADY
BEING AN INN
IN 1722
A.D.

Sign outside the Royal Oak, Chesterfield.

guest house belonging to the Knights Templar, but aside from this none of the pubs in Derbyshire claim such an early foundation.

After the Dissolution of the Monasteries, brewing became a largely secular activity. Brewing for domestic consumption remained in the hands of housewives, while inns, taverns and alehouses brewed beer on the premises to serve their customers. A survey of 1577 showed that in Derbyshire there were 276 ale houses, 18 inns and five taverns.

Few of these 16th century inns still exist, and we have little information about their operation. A notable exception, however, is the Hardwick Inn at Doe Lea near Chesterfield. Inventories and other documents give us some idea of the brewing process at the inn. Water was heated in a large copper. It was then let into a large wooden tub containing malt and roasted barley. This mixture was stirred for an hour or two and the liquor was then run off to produce ale. If beer was being produced, hops were added to provide flavour and improve its keeping properties. The resulting liquid was then strained through a horse-hair sieve into another wooden tub where yeast was added and fermentation began. This process usually lasted for about three days, after which the beer was transferred into wooden barrels to await a further period of fermentation. When this was complete, the barrels were sealed with a wooden bung and stored on beer thralls or trestles. When ready for drinking, it was drawn from the barrel and served directly to customers in pewter tankards.

Large scale brewing continued in the grand country houses such as Haddon, Hardwick, Chatsworth and Calke as well as some of the smaller local manor houses. In the smaller houses, the bake-house or scullery often served as a brewery. In larger establishments there was a separate brewhouse where great quantities of ale were brewed once or twice a month. In the 1740s a considerable sum was spent on setting up the brewhouse at Calke Abbey. This was connected to the ale and beer cellars of the house by a brick tunnel, with a steep slope, down which the barrels could easily be rolled. The brewer was an important member of staff in the larger households, but because of the obvious links with yeast it was not uncommon for one man to fulfil the roles of both baker and brewer. Sir Henry Crewe of Calke Abbey employed such a man but in 1815 complained about both his beer and his brewer. 'You never see a drop sparkle in the glass and it tastes thick and sweet,' exclaimed Sir Henry. 'What I like is a fine light ale; small beer should be brisk and fresh but not tart.' As for the brewer, he described him as, 'the man who has spoiled all my beer for the last three years!'

In these large houses the brewhouse was often located near to the stables because of the strong smell. At Chatsworth the beer was piped into the house from the brewhouse in the stable block. Unfortunately, the pipe ran under the 'Conservative Wall' of the hot house and it was rumoured that more than one enterprising gardener tapped into the supply for his own personal use.

Stage Coach (after Pynn).

By the 18th century Derby was beginning to gain a reputation for the quality of its ale. Daniel Defoe wrote that, 'The trade of the town is chiefly in good malt and good ale; nor is the quantity of the latter unreasonably small, which as they say, they dispose of among themselves, though they spare some for their neighbours also'. Celia Fiennes, visiting Chesterfield only a few years earlier, however, commented that, 'in this town is the best ale in the kingdom generally esteemed'. This period also saw the establishment and growth of a number of coaching inns throughout the county. These were places that stabled teams of horses for stage coaches and mail coaches and replaced tired teams with fresh ones. Traditionally they were often 10 to 15 miles apart but the actual distance was dependent on the terrain. Some of the larger towns had as many as 10 such inns and competition between them was intense, not only for the income from the stagecoach operators but also for the money they received for food and drink supplied to the wealthy passengers.

In Derby, coaching inns included the Bell, the George, the Tiger, the Red Lion, the White Lion, the Angel, the Cross Keys and many more. Only the Bell, the Tiger and the George (now Jorrocks) still survive. At Chesterfield the two principal coaching inns were the Angel and the Star. Pigott's Directory of 1835 records the following services leaving from or calling at the Angel:

> To LONDON, the *Royal Mail* (from Leeds) every morning at half past two; goes through Melton Mowbray, Kettering, &c – the Express, every

afternoon at a quarter before four – the Courier, every night at eight - and the Royal Hope (from Halifax) every afternoon at one; all go thro' Nottingham, Leicester, Northampton, Woburn &c.

To BIRMINGHAM, the Royal Mail, and Quicksilver (from Sheffield) every morning at nine; both go through Alfreton, Derby, Lichfield, & - and the Telegraph (from Leeds) every day at twelve (Sunday excepted); goes thro' Belper, Derby, Burton-upon-Trent, Lichfield &c.

To HALIFAX, the Royal Hope (from London) every day at twelve; goes through Sheffield, Huddersfield, &c.

To LEEDS, the Royal Mail and the Courier (from London) every day at twelve – and the Express, every forenoon at eleven; all go through Sheffield, Barnsley, Wakefield, &c. – and the Telegraph (from Birmingham) every afternoon at two; goes the same route

To MANCHESTER, the Champion (from Nottingham) every morning (Sunday excepted) at ten; goes through Baslow, Stoney Middleton, Chapel-en-le-frith, and Stockport

To NOTTINGHAM and NEWARK, the Champion (from Manchester) every afternoon at 3; goes thro' Mansfield &c.

To SHEFFIELD, the Royal Mail (from Birmingham) every day at twelve – the Quicksilver, every afternoon at four – and the Traveller, every morning (Sunday excepted) at eight.

Similar coaching inns sprang up throughout the county at places such as Alfreton, Ashbourne, Bakewell, Belper, Buxton, Chesterfield, Winster and Wirksworth. Some of these, such as the Lion at Belper and the Red Lion at Wirksworth, still survive but others have passed into the landscape of the Christmas card and the romantic novel.

In their heyday these coaching inns were busy and bustling places, full of excitement. Joseph Hatton, the 19th-century writer and journalist, described the arrival of the mail at the Angel in Chesterfield in the following manner:

'Presently from the eastern corner of the Market Place, came toiling along the mail coach from London to Manchester – a picture of light, life and elegance. A whip flourished harmlessly over the steaming cattle. A horn blown merrily behind; a flash of red and gold and black and silver, and the coach pulled up in front of the Angel window; there was a rush of grooms and stable-helps; and luggage, horses and passengers almost together, poured into the inn yard, and in less than five minutes a fresh team was harnessed.'

The Lion at Belper.

By the 18th and 19th centuries, inns and taverns throughout the county were not just places to enjoy a drink but were also important commercial and social centres used for meetings, entertainment, sales, auctions and inquests. Friendly societies and the early trade unions met here and even the first co-op store in Derby was established in the yard of the George Inn. Bodies were laid out here prior to burial and some inns even provided hearses for hire! In 1822 the George Inn at Alfreton advertised, 'Neat Post Chaises and good Horses with careful drivers, hearse and Mourning Coaches with Black or Grey Horses'.

Soldiers were frequently billeted in public houses, although the rates paid by the military were far from generous. In 1706 Joseph Broughton, the Mayor of Derby, wrote to Thomas Coke MP asking him to get billeted troops removed from the town because the innkeepers were 'all losers'. Four decades later in 1745 the Scottish soldiers of Bonnie Prince Charlie found billets in local inns and taverns as well as private houses in the town but made no payment whatsoever! Over half a century later, in 1813, an Act was passed providing that an inn keeper should receive 10 pence for a day's billet, for which he must provide the soldier with a hot dinner. Despite this legislation, the 'Soldiers Room' at most of the principal inns remained a model of discomfort and sometimes squalor. That at the Bell Inn in Sadler Gate was reached from a stable-yard by a flight of stone steps, below which was a large open pigsty. The King's Head was no better but a contemporary account suggested that the New Inn afforded better quarters.

But inns also acted as official and unofficial recruiting offices for both the army and the Royal Navy. In June 1795 the following notice appeared in *The Derby Mercury*:

'WANTED AS VOLUNTEERS
FOR THE
COUNTY OF DERBY
To serve in the ROYAL NAVY during the WAR and for three months after the respective ships shall arrive in any port of Great Britain; A NUMBER of ABLE and ORDINARY SEAMEN and ABLE BODIED LANDSMEN, from the age of 16 to 45 years to whom a very handsome bounty will be given by the County, one third to be paid at the time of Enrolment and the other two-thirds on joining any of His Majesty's Ships. All such Able Bodied Men who are willing to serve their country may apply at the Rendezvous, George inn, Derby, where a Navy Officer will attend to receive them. They will, on being enrolled enter into immediate Pay according to their abilities (part of which may be remitted for Use of their Wives and Families) and be entitles to the usual advantage of Prize Money &c, &c
GOD save the KING and Constitution'

The local militia also used public houses to aid recruitment. In August 1796 the following notice was placed in *The Derby Mercury*:

'DERBY MILITIA
A few likely YOUNG MEN are WANTED as substitutes to complete the above militia. Any person willing to engage may apply to Serjeant STANSBY at the Tiger in King Street, Derby'

Several of the larger and grander inns hosted dinners and assemblies. These assemblies were an essential feature of the formal Georgian social scene and were held regularly throughout the year or during a restricted season. The most important element was an evening ball, during which several formal set dances took place. In addition, card games were played at side tables or in adjacent rooms and a great deal of conversation and gossip exchanged. The Angel Inn at Chesterfield held regular winter assemblies. A poster dated 1816 announced four assemblies for the period November 1816 to February 1817. The subscription for all four assemblies was 10s 6d and included tea and sandwiches. Dancing commenced at 9pm and would have provided an opportunity for the eligible bachelors to meet young ladies of the town.

The Green Man Hotel, Ashbourne.

Similar events were held at inns throughout the county. The Blackmoor's Head at Ashbourne held dinners to celebrate the King's birthday, military victories and other significant local events. It also hosted a number of assemblies and advertised itself as the resort of the town's card and dancing assemblies. Visiting in 1789, John Byng noted that the inn yard was, 'crowded by chaises full of company going to a grand dinner in this town; there to be overwhelmed by dress, compliments, hams and fowls, ducks, custards and trifles; losing their time, their peace; and not improving their politeness'! Dancing Masters regularly visited inns at Derby, Chesterfield, Wirksworth, Duffield and Ashbourne. In 1803 Messrs Tunaley and Fritch engaged a room at the Green Man in Ashbourne and charged one guinea entry and one guinea per quarter. Ladies also needed their hair dressed in order to look their best at these assemblies. Hairdressers used public houses as a base to serve their local clientele and advertised their services in the local press. In October 1785, Mr Henshaw established himself at the Black's Head to cater for the needs of the ladies of Ashbourne.

From time to time other tradesmen also based themselves at public houses and advertised their services in local newspapers. From the middle of the 19th century, these included photographers. More and more middle-class families were keen to have a portrait of themselves or their family and a growing band of professional photographers were ready to meet this demand. Before specialist studios had become available, some of the more respectable inns were the obvious place for these photographic portraits to be taken. In June 1854 *The Derbyshire Times* contained the following notice:

'MR R N HARROP
PHOTOGRAPHIC ARTIST
FROM MANCHESTER
Will be taking these beautiful PORTRAITS at the Angel Inn, Chesterfield
on and after June 19th for a very short time.'

Public houses were regularly the focus of public rejoicing. At Alfreton, following the defeat of Napoleon, a meeting was held at the George Inn on 6th June 1814 when the following resolution was passed: 'That Public rejoicing do take place on Tuesday 14th inst and that the day be ushered in by the ringing of bells and firing of cannon. That the inhabitants be regaled with Roast Beef and Plum Pudding and sufficient quantity of ale, that such dinner be cold and partaken of in the field adjoining the George Inn if the day prove favourable, but if wet set out in the various public houses ... admission by ticket obtainable from the committee. NB it is hoped that every inhabitant (not excepting the women) will take part. That the committee purchase a fat ox and two sheep, that the tower of the Church be brilliantly illuminated, that two bands of music be engaged for the day and that subscription be made immediately to cover expenses ... That there shall be a dinner at the George Inn on the same day for the gentlemen of the Town and the neighbourhood'. Tickets for the dinner, including wine were priced at 15 shillings each. Just a few years later, in 1821, the Coronation of George IV was met with rejoicing throughout the whole kingdom and pubs played their part in this. *The Derby Mercury* reported that at Alfreton following a day of celebrations 'a party of 70 sat down to an excellent dinner at the George' and the evening concluded with a ball at the Angel.

But not all classes of society were able to join in such celebrations. Unemployment, poverty and harsh laws led to unrest in many parts of the country. It was within this climate of poverty, anger, repression and despair that the 'Pentrich Revolution' was briefly fought and lost. The detailed planning for this uprising took place at the White Horse Inn at Pentrich. It was here that Jeremiah Brandreth, the leader of the rebels, briefed his followers, giving them instructions and promising that he would lead them to bread, beef, beer and glory. With the aid of a map, he showed them the route they would take towards Nottingham and eventually London. On the night of 9 June 1817 upwards of 300 men from Pentrich and the surrounding areas marched on London in the mistaken belief that they were part of a great national working-class uprising. The rebels paused at several pubs on the road through Ripley and Codnor where they gained more recruits. At the Old Glasshouse Inn at Codnor, Brandreth refused to pay for the bread, cheese and ale, declaring that after the rebellion a Bank of England note would be worthless! Inevitably the venture was doomed to failure. This ragged band of revolutionaries began to dwindle when the expected support failed to materialise and only about 40 remained when a detachment of hussars routed them at Giltbrook in Nottinghamshire. Thirty were arrested, including Brandreth, who, with two others, was hanged at Derby a few months later. Later in the same month Ann Weightman, the licensee of the White Horse, was convicted of having permitted a seditious meeting to be held. As a consequence, her licence to sell ale was forfeited. Shortly afterwards the inn was demolished on the orders of the Duke of Devonshire.

Sparring bouts were commonly held in taverns and inns throughout the county. In 1860 *The Derby Mercury* newspaper advertised: 'A Grand Sparring Treat at George Whitman's Noah's Ark Inn, Morledge, Derby'. These contests were bare knuckle fights that sometimes went on for several hours. Other entertainment included bear baiting, dog fighting and cock fighting. This latter pastime attracted all classes of society and the local gentry and aristocracy sometimes placed large bets on the outcome. Cock fighting involved cockerels being trained to fight other cocks to the death, often aided by sharp spurs attached to their legs. Substantial bets were placed on the outcome of individual battles or a series called a 'main'. The action took place in a cockpit, a small sunken area with space for spectators ranged around. The cocks were weighed in before the contest and introduced to the ring by their trainers or 'feeders' In Ashbourne the main cockpit was at the Blackmoor's Head. It was here in the 1750s that regular three-day matches were held in May each year between Hugo Meynell of Bradley and Sir Charles Sedley of Nutall. Both were renowned sporting gentlemen and the stakes at these events were very high – 20 guineas for the winner of each individual battle and no less than 400 guineas for the winner of the whole contest! Similar sporting matches, though on a smaller scale, were held at inn yards throughout the county and were often advertised in the local press.

But times changed. Cock fighting was abolished in 1835 and in 1868 William Hull of the Horse and Jockey at Cow Hill near Belper was refused a renewal of his licence for not conducting his house in a proper manner. A local newspaper reported that he had been found to have established a rat pit at the premises, where terriers were set upon a number of rats. Bets were placed on how quickly the dog could despatch all of the creatures. The same newspaper account declared that this was a lucrative sport to attract the betting fraternity!

Other pastimes were of a more civilised nature. In 1751 a Florists' Feast was held at the Royal Oak in the Market Place, Derby, for the 'Show of Auriculas', where the first half guinea was won by Mr Grainger's June. The second prize went to Mr Thomas Bennett, who also won the prize for the best polyanthus. The local newspaper reported that the show was, 'the greatest collection of flowers ever seen'. Also, in Derby, the Society of Musicians met every third week at the Tiger in King Street where it provided beer for its members. Elsewhere in the county the Alfreton Horticultural Society held its regular meetings at the George Inn. These featured competitions with prizes in a number of different classes, including a variety of flowers, herbaceous plants, fruits and vegetables. At Crich an annual Carnation Show was held at the King's Arms. In 1782 Mr William Breffitt, Head Gardener to George Morewood Esq, won the Pickatee Prize with the Blood Royal Pickatee. Similar floral and horticultural shows were held at pubs in many parts of the county. At Derby, strolling players frequently performed at inns,

The White Hart at West Hallam.

especially at fair times, and there are records of such shows taking place at both the Virgin and the George.

In rural areas public houses were sometimes the meeting place for cow clubs. On payment of a regular sum (typically one shilling per cow) farmers were entitled to free veterinary service and advice. There are records of such clubs in a number of pubs including the White Hart and the Newdigate Arms, both at West Hallam.

Important commercial business was often conducted at these inns. Meetings of the Derby Canal Company were held at the Bell Inn for a number of years and in 1834 a public meeting was held there to discuss a possible rail link to Derby. A few years earlier on 14 March 1799 a notice was given of a meeting to be held at the Bulls Head at Crich by the trustees of the Cromford to Langley Mill Turnpike to consider the propriety of erecting a chain or side gate on a road leading to the turnpike between Bullbridge and the Tollbar House.

Sales, auctions and bankruptcy hearings were held at many of the inns within the county and notices of these appear regularly in the pages of *The Derby Mercury* newspaper. On 25 July 1799 *The Derby Mercury* contained the following notice: 'The creditors of Mr Wm. Hickson are desired to attend at the Glass House Inn at Codnor on Saturday next at 2 o'clock in the afternoon to consider the proper mode of disposing of the crops on the farm at Knowts Hall and for the purpose to agree a value fixed thereon or to appoint proper persons to determine such value.'

The Bell Inn Derby.

A wide range of lots were regularly auctioned at inns throughout Derbyshire. These ranged from household furniture to livestock, property, public houses, breweries and even whole estates. In March 1802 an auction was held at the George Hotel, Alfreton. Among the lots advertised for sale was 'the Manor of Newland in the parish of Alfreton'. This comprised 'good buildings' and 188 acres of land. It was advertised a being tythe free and containing valuable coal and limestone deposits.

For much of the 18th and 19th centuries the public house also played an important role in the administration of local justice. In many parts of Derbyshire the pub or inn was the only readily available large indoor space where public judicial business could take place. As a consequence, petty sessions (the forerunners of magistrates' courts) and coroners courts were frequently held in public houses. The proceedings were usually held in an upstairs or back room of the pub, sometimes with their own entrance so that the magistrate or coroner did not have to pass through the beery throng. Pub justice was also a lucrative business for the landlord, who benefitted from payment for the room, as well as increased custom which petty sessions and coroners' courts brought.

Courts of Petty Sessions were introduced in the 18th century. They were presided over by an individual Justice of the Peace and dealt with minor cases such as drunkenness, poaching and vagrancy. These Justices of the Peace were usually local landowners of some standing and frequently held court in a 'Justice Room' in their own home. This, however, was not always the case and Petty Sessions were sometimes held in a public house. There is evidence that the Green Man and Blackmoor's Head Royal Hotel at Ashbourne and the Royal Oak in Chapel en le Frith were both used for this purpose.

Public houses were also used as a venue for a much older form of justice. *The Derby Mercury* of 26 September 1860 contained the following notice:

MANORS OF HEAGE, ALDERWASLEY AND ASHLEYHAY, BONSALL, WIRKSWORTH, IRETON WOOD AND MATLOCK. Notice is hereby GIVEN that the COURT LEET and VIEW OF

FRANKPLEDGE with the GREAT COURTS BARON of the LORDS of the above MANORS will be held at the undermentioned times and places, viz: - HEAGE at the WHITE HART INN on WEDNESDAY 3rd October; ALDERWASLEY and ASHLEYHAY at the BEAR INN, ALDERWASLEY on THURSDAY 4th October; BONSALL at the KING'S HEAD INN on THURSDAY 11th October; WIRKSWORTH at the MOOT HALL on MONDAY 15th October; IRETON WOOD at the RED LION INN, WIRKSWORTH on MONDAY 15th OCTOBER; MATLOCK at the WHEAT SHEAF INN on MONDAY 22nd OCTOBER

These manorial courts dated back to the Middle Ages and were periodic meetings of tenants convened and presided over by the Lord of the Manor or his steward, who was usually a man of some substance and often trained in law. They dealt with a range of judicial and administrative matters such as the transfer of property and the supervision of common land. They might also enquire into the state of watercourses, roads, paths and ditches to guard against encroachment. The court also offered arbitration in disputes between individuals over issues such as debt, trespass or breach of an agreement.

During the Victorian period, coroner's inquests were frequently held in public houses. They provided a large enough space to view the body and were able to accommodate the jury of 12 as well as the coroner and witnesses. Reports of these inquests were widely reported in the local press. *The Derbyshire Times and Chesterfield Reporter* published, on 6 April 1870, recorded the following account of an inquest into a fatal accident:

'On Saturday evening an inquest was held at the Dog and Doublet, Pye Bridge by Coroner, Mr Busby, touching on the death of Daniel Severn, a ganger employed by Messrs Oakes of the Alfreton Coal and Ironworks. On Friday afternoon the deceased was driving three horses drawing a number of empty wagons to the Old Deep Pit for the purpose of getting them filled with coal. On the way he found that a loaded truck was obstructing the road and endeavoured to stop his horses, but could not. He got between his wagons and the truck, and was seriously crushed. Assistance was immediately rendered and he was carried home. Mr Fielding, surgeon of Alfreton was sent for, and on his arrival, with his assistant, found that the deceased had suffered internal injuries and that the case was a hopeless one. He remained with him up to the time of his death, which took place the same night. The jury returned a verdict of accidental death.'

In the mining areas of the county many of the inquests were concerned with colliery accidents, but in May 1896 at the Plough Inn at Brackenfield the same Coroner swore in a jury to conduct an inquest into the violent death of Miss Elizabeth Boot. She had been found at a local barn, lying on her back, with a gash to her throat five inches long. The floor of the barn was covered in blood and a bloodstained billhook lay discarded nearby. A certain William Pugh, an unemployed collier, was suspected of causing the death, and after considering the evidence, including the findings of a rather gruesome post mortem examination, a verdict of wilful murder was returned. Pugh was found guilty at a subsequent trail and sentenced to be hanged only a few weeks later. But this was not the end of the story. The scene of the crime attracted a great deal of ghoulish interest and many of these visitors were accommodated in local hostelries!

At a time when there was no organised police force in the country, societies for the prosecution of felons were established in many parts of the country. These were societies in which each member paid a subscription into a joint fund which was used to offer a reward, cover the cost of catching the criminal and bringing them to trial and sometimes providing compensation for any stolen items. There were several such societies in Derbyshire and meetings were frequently held in local inns. On 28 February 1799, for example, *The Derby Mercury* gave notice of the annual meeting of the South Wingfield Association for the Prosecution of Felons to be held at the Peacock, Oakerthorpe. The same newspaper had previously reported that the Association had agreed to the following awards to be granted to an informer for evidence leading to a conviction for the following crimes:

£5 5s 0d for burglary or highway robbery

£3 3s 0d for stealing a horse, or a cow or a pig or any other capital offence

10s 0d for stealing utensils or peas, bean, cabbages, etc or any
other petty larceny

It was not unknown for pubs to also be the scenes of crime ranging from murder and assault to burglary, prostitution and illegal gambling. Pages of the local newspapers abound with examples. In Derby many of the cases brought before the local magistrate's courts were for drunk and disorderly behaviour. An unusual example of such a case was reported in *The Derby Mercury* in February 1878 when John McCormick was summoned by Bridget McCormick for unlawfully assaulting her at the Durham Ox public house. The defendant was the complainant's husband but the case was dismissed because they were living apart and the defendant had frequently appealed to the police for protection from the violence of his wife!

At a time when there was the death penalty for over 100 crimes, public executions drew large crowds and provided good business for public houses, particularly in Derby where many hangings took place. The place of execution was outside the town gaol in Friargate. It seems likely that the various pubs on the roads into the town as well as the area around Friargate would have been particularly busy on execution days. According to local legend, the Greyhound Inn was where the prisoner paused for his last drink before his 'last drop'!

Public houses, particularly in towns, also played an important role in the political life of the period. At a time when bribery was commonplace in the conduct of elections, large bills were frequently run up by parliamentary candidates to treat their potential supporters to food and drink. In 1761 Sir Henry Harpur was returned as one of the members of parliament for Derbyshire. He paid for drinks in many of the pubs in Derby in the hope and anticipation of influencing the electors in his favour. A broadsheet published at the time detailed 45 public houses under the heading 'List of Houses enjoyed for the Entertainment of Friends of Sir Henry Harpur at the time of the Election'.

Pubs were also used to treat the supporters of victorious candidates. In August 1830 Lord George Henry Cavendish and Mr Mundy were elected unopposed to represent Derbyshire in the House of Commons. *The Derby Mercury* reported that, 'At four o'clock various Inns, Taverns and Public Houses were opened for the reception of the respective friends of the newly returned members. The houses opened by Lord G H Cavendish were the King's Head, the New Inn and the County Tavern. Those occupied by the friends of Mr Mundy were the Bell Inn, the Tyger, the Royal Oak, the Fox and Owl and the Rose and Crown. Lord George and Mr Mundy presided at their separate inns. The parties at each of the houses were very numerous, the dinners were excellent; the wines &c were furnished in unfailing profusion; the toasts were patriotic and very appropriate to the occasion. The conviviality was kept up everywhere to a late hour but propriety and decorum were the order of the evening.'

Some of these election campaigns, however, were far from peaceful. Only a few decades later in November 1868 violence erupted during the general election campaign in Clay Cross. Pitched battles were fought in and around many of the pubs in the town and it took several hours for order to be restored. It seems that the rioters were largely local miners (who supported the Liberals). They were worried about an increase in support for the Conservative candidates. The New Inn was one of the first pubs to be attacked because it was the location of a Conservative Committee Room. The windows were all smashed with what a contemporary account described as 'stones and brick ends going through like hail'. The mob then moved on to attack the Queen's Hotel, the Prince of Wales and the Buck. Order was eventually restored, although 50 members of the Birmingham Borough Police Force had to be drafted in to assist 20 members of the Derbyshire County Constabulary already on duty there.

Public houses were also involved in the wider political issues of the day. In 1813 a meeting of the clergy of Derby and neighbourhood took place at the King's Head Inn to resist the movement in favour of repealing the disabilities of the Roman Catholics.

Some of the more respectable inns also played an important role in civic occasions. The opening of the assizes was always marked by a banquet. In March 1751 *The Derby Mercury* reported that Sir Thomas Greasley of Drakelow, the High Sheriff, accompanied by a great number of gentlemen and tradesmen 'and attended by several servants in Handsome, gold Lac'd Liveries came to the King's Head at Derby before going to meet the judge of the Assizes'. On a number of occasions in the early years of the 20th century, the Corporation of Chesterfield entertained the Mayor at the Portland Hotel in the town.

Many of the early trade unions and friendly societies held their meetings in public houses. These organisations offered conviviality and mutual protection in uncertain times, and provided a range of benefits such as insurance against sickness, old age and death. In 1797, for example, members of the society at the Nag's Head in Chesterfield paid a monthly subscription of 1s as well as 2d for expenses. According to a survey published in the same year, 'Persons who have been registered members for two years are allowed weekly, in the case of sickness, 8s a week during one year; and if they

The Spread Eagle, Etwall. The Independent Order of Oddfellows met here.

continue ill a longer time, 5s a week during the remainder of their illness. From £2 to £5 are allowed towards the funeral of a member. A member on the death of his wife, receives from each brother member 6d.' Some of these organisations were more akin to secret societies or masonic lodges. At Etwall the Independent Order of Oddfellows held their meetings at the Spread Eagle. These were conducted in a room behind a bolted door guarded by a 'Tyler' and were presided over by a chairman known as a 'Noble Grand'. From time to time it seems that he struggled to keep order and fines were imposed for such offences as 'fighting, disgraceful conduct, being drunk, quarrelling and swearing in Lodge'. In 1867 five brothers were fined for 'Insulting the Noble Grand'. Although there was an important social element to these meetings, members enjoyed significant benefits. In return for a fortnightly contribution of a few pence, brethren could expect sick pay, the services of a surgeon and ultimately a funeral donation.

Pubs also hosted meetings of some of the more radical elements of the Labour movement. In April 1839 the Brampton and Chesterfield United Radical Association (a Chartist organisation) was formed after meetings had been held in the Turf Tavern at Holywell Cross and the Red Lion at Brampton. The purpose of this organisation was to support the movement for the People's Charter, a document that made a number of demands including universal suffrage, a secret ballot, equal constituencies and payment for MPs.

By 1861 trade unionism was well established and in that year the UK First Annual Trade Directory listed the following trade unions meeting in public houses in Derby:

Boot and shoemakers	Buck in the Park, Friargate
Bookbinder's Consolidated Union	Rose and Thistle, Chapel Street
Boilermakers	Lamb Inn, Park Street
Brush makers	Nelson Inn, Wardwick
Cabinet Makers	Half Moon Inn, Sadler Gate
Carpenters	Bulls Head, Queen Street
Coachbuilders	Green Man Inn, St Peters Churchyard
Compositors and Printers	Buck in the Park, Friargate
Amalgamated Engineers	New Inn, King Street
Engine Drivers	Red Lion, Canal Street
Iron Moulders	Talbot Inn, Irongate
United Order of Smiths	Bull's Head, Queen Street
Tailors	White Hart, Bridge Street
Ribbon Weavers	Dove Tavern, Nunn Street

These pubs provided a vital service to fledgling union branches. They were often the only place available for hire and constituted the union's meeting place, hotel, library, post office and job centre. In some trades, workmen moved around looking for work and the pub might provide accommodation as well as details of any work available locally. In some cases, the landlord would act as a banker, holding and perhaps dispensing union funds and benefits, although as the years passed these responsibilities fell more and more upon the branch secretary.

In the decades that followed, public houses continued to be places where a friendly society or local trade union branch might meet and important decisions were sometimes made here. At Chesterfield the Three Tuns was used for the 1861 meeting that brought the South Yorkshire Miners' Association into Derbyshire; and the Freemasons Arms on Newbold Road hosted the first delegate meeting of colliery lodges, which led to the formation of the North Derbyshire Miners' Association. Towards the end of the century the Queen's Head was the venue chosen for the formation of a Trades Council, which brought together members of a number of trade unions in the area.

Freemasons also established some of their early lodges in public houses. They founded their first Derby lodge as early as 1732 and held their meetings at the Virgin Inn. Shortly after they moved to the George Inn and summons to Lodge meetings were placed in the local press. The following notice from 1787 was placed in *The Derby Mercury* and is typical:

'TYRIAN LODGE DERBY
On Monday the 16th September inst. will be a Meeting of the most ancient and honourable society of FREE and ACCEPTED MASONS at the George Inn
Sir J B WARREN, Bart P.G.M.
The Company of every brother will be esteemed a favour
Dinner on table at half past two'

By the latter years of the 18th century they had moved again. This time to the Tiger in the Cornmarket. In 1859 the Beaurepaire Freemasons Lodge was inaugurated at the New Inn at Belper when the Marquis of Hastings was installed as the first Worshipful Master. At Chesterfield the Scarsdale Lodge held their annual dinner at the newly opened Portland Hotel in 1901.

Professional men also used public houses to meet clients and conduct their business. Local newspapers of the period contain frequent notices from doctors visiting the area and advertising their services to the more affluent members of society. In 1777 Mr Pegg of Breadsall held consultations at the Seven Stars every Friday and Fair

Day concerning his, 'infallible remedy for consumption'. Some years later a notice in *The Derby Mercury* announced that, 'DR LAMBERT (Of the London Medical Establishment, Bristol) … has received many requests to visit Derbyshire: he has made arrangements to do so though other pressing engagements oblige him to stay only a short time at each place. Those persons who have honoured him with invitations as well as others labouring under diseases will take notice that he will be at Belper, at the George Inn Thurs Dec. 4th from 1 o' clock noon to 9 (pm) Alfreton, at the George Inn Fri. Dec. 5th from 9 in the morning to 2 (p.m.) Chesterfield at the Angel Inn Fri 5th. Dec. from 5 in the evening to 9 (p.m.) and Sat. Dec. 6th from 9 in the morning to 9 (p.m.)'

Vets also used public houses to conduct their business and treat their patients. An advertisement in *The Derby Mercury* announced that 'John Fowke the famous cow doctor from Kilburn is now removed from the Saracen's Head to the Bell where his drinks are to be had at any time'. The breeding of horses and other animals was sometimes arranged at public houses. *The Derby Mercury* of 4 March 1747 contained the following notice:

> This is to inform the PUBLICK that there is now in the hands of ROBERT FELL at the King's head in DUFFIELD near DERBY a fine Dapple Grey Ston'd Horse, Fifteen Hands and One Inch high and free from all Blemishes: He is allow'd by all gentlemen who are good Judges, to be as beautiful and strong a horse of his kind as any in England. He will leap at Half a Guinea a Mare for the season; the money to be paid down at the Stable Door…all persons who are disposed to bring their Mares and make use of him will be carefully attended.'

A similar advertisement announced that, 'there is now at the Blue Boar on Nun's Green a high bred Berkshire Boar that will brim sows at reasonable rates'.

The 19th century also saw a massive and rapid increase in the population of many towns and cities. Hundreds of thousands of people flocked from the countryside to find employment in mills, foundries and factories. In Derby, as in other towns, people often lived in overcrowded and squalid conditions and their only escape was the local pub. In addition to beer and good company, the pub also provided a range of activities including darts, quoits, billiards, dominoes and skittles. But not everyone approved of such goings on. As early as 1786 the Mayor of Derby complained that 'apprentices are permitted to play cards, dice, billiards, skittles and other kinds of gambling' in the public houses. Almost a century later in 1861 three constables were cautioned for having played dominoes at the Flying Dutchman beer house in Chesterfield, even though they were off duty and claimed that they were not playing for money!

In mining areas it was the pub that provided the place where miners met to be paid their wages by the 'butty' (sub-contractor). This practice was not always popular with their wives, who feared that wages might be drunk away before food and household expenses were accounted for. In 1833, however, Parliament enacted legislation prohibiting the paying of wages in public houses. Many of these 19th-century town pubs were swept away by post-war slum clearance and redevelopment but some still remain. In Derby these include the Furnace, the Maypole, the Brick and Tile and the Royal Standard. In Chesterfield the Victoria Inn at Brampton and the

The Royal Standard, now the Brewery Tap.

Tramway Tavern nearer the centre of the town still attract a local clientele.

A variety of entertainment was provided in these inns. In Derby, strolling players performed at inns and public houses especially at fair times and there are records of such performances taking place at the Virgin Inn in the Market Place and the George in Sadler Gate. In Belper in May 1825 the Spencer and Tunidigen Company of Comedians showed off their talents at the George and Dragon Inn. Elsewhere in the town the Holloways, a theatrical company, frequently pitched their tent in the inn yard of the Tiger. Shows of wild beasts, the forerunners of circuses, also took place in the yards of public houses. A notice dated 26 July 1753 invited people to view, 'a Grand Collection of Living wild Creatures; at the Anchor on the Gaol Bridge'. Having just arrived in England the show included 'The Magnanimous King of the Beasts, a great HE-Lyon taken near the City of Bassora in the Kingdom of Persia'. There was also a He-Leopard and a she-leopard from Senegal and Turkey respectively. It was claimed that the hyaenas could imitate human voices and lure natives out of their huts and then devour them. Eight years earlier a similar show was held at the Blackmoor's Head in Full Street. At Etwall it is said that an elephant was stabled at the Hawk and Buckle when a circus visited the area. But not all animal exhibitions were quite so unusual or spectacular. In 1790 an American Elk was displayed for two days in a room at the Red Lion in Derby. The animal was en-route to London to be viewed by the King. Admittance was charged at six pence for ladies and gentlemen and three pence for children and servants. Pubs were also used as a venue for more intellectual and educational activities. The Green Man at Ashbourne was the venue for occasional lectures. In 1783, for example, Mr South gave a series of lectures on 'Natural and experimental Philosophy, astronomy etc'.

Race meetings at Derby and Chesterfield also brought increased custom to the inns and taverns in these towns. At Derby the first recorded race meeting was held in 1733. A Race Ball was held for the gentry in the Assembly Rooms but the following evening a similar event was held for the townspeople at the Virgin Inn. Similar celebrations were held during race weeks in Chesterfield. In 1800, on the first night of the races, the Duke of Devonshire provided a cold collation at the ball held in the assembly room of the Virgin Inn. Betting on horses gradually became more popular with a wider range of society, and in 1856 on race days the Clerk of the Course held court at the King's Head in Derby where all stakes and forfeits were to be paid 'before eleven o' clock of the forenoon on the day of the running'. There was no on-course betting at that time so those wishing to place bets would also have helped boost the profits of the landlord.

The Industrial Revolution of the 18th and 19th centuries also brought the canals and then railways. A number of canal-side inns were built to serve the needs of boatmen as well as lock keepers, labourers and others who worked to keep these 18th-century arteries of trade moving. Visiting the Navigation Inn at Shardlow in 1782, Pastor Moritz, a German traveller, complained about the behaviour of the bargees. 'A wilder,

The Navigation Inn, Shardlow.

The New Inn, Shardlow.

coarser type of men than those I met gathered in the kitchen of this inn I have never seen,' he declared. 'Their speech, their clothing, their appearance – all were rough and their language even more dreadful. Hardly a word came out of their mouths without a "God damn me!" to it; and so with blaspheming, brawling and cursing, the time went on.' Not surprisingly, having supped he hurried off to bed but his sleep was disturbed by the bargees 'roaring and raving nearly all of the night'. When he got up in the morning, however, he noted that 'there was not one of them to be seen or heard'. The Navigation Inn still exists at Shardlow as well as the New Inn and the Old Crown, which also date from this period. One of the canal warehouses in the village has also been converted into a pub. Previously named Hoskin's Wharf, it is now known as the Clock Warehouse.

From the mid-19th century, canals began to be replaced by railways and a number of railway inns were built to serve the people who travelled on them. In Derby the Midland Hotel was one of the earliest railway hotels in the world. Built in 1839, it catered for the nobility and the gentry as well as other first-class passengers, and it was here that Queen Victoria stayed the night in 1849. Food and accommodation were of the highest standards and the quality of its wine cellar matched the sophisticated pallet of its most wealthy and discerning clients.

Just a few hundred yards away from the Midland Hotel stands the Brunswick Inn. This was built in 1841 and served second-class passengers, railway workers and the growing band of commercial travellers who used the railways to ply their wares. It offered a more basic fare and its charges were considerably less than those in the Midland. A plain breakfast could be had for 1s 6d and dinner cost just two shillings.

The difference between these two establishments was summed up at the time by the comment that that the conversation in the Midland Hotel was of 'hunting and shooting' whilst the talk in the Brunswick Inn was of 'shunting and hooting'!

Both establishments benefitted from their links to the North Midland Railway, for in 1843 the company decreed that, 'the Proprietor of the Midland Hotel... and the leasees of the Brunswick Inn... shall have the exclusive privilege of sending porters on the station platform to solicit the custom of passengers to their respective premises'. Conscious of maintaining their own reputation, the company also added the caveat that the parties were to 'conduct themselves with civility and propriety in all respects'!

Elsewhere in the county other public houses were built close to railway stations to serve the needs of businessmen and travelling salesmen. In Chesterfield the Station Hotel, Commercial Hotel and Midland Hotel all served this function. The Station Hotel also catered for the growing popularity of cycling and proclaimed that every security was provided for cyclists' machines with the town guide stating that 'tourists on wheels largely patronise the establishment during the season'. The Great Northern Hotel at Mickleover was built around 1878. It served the newly built railway station on the Company's Friargate Line extension to Egginton Junction. Other railway inns in Derbyshire include those at Belper and Matlock Bath.

The Great Northern Hotel, Mickleover.

Although coach travel had given way to the railways, local carriers continued to provide an essential service linking the railways with local shops and businesses. A network developed which was focussed on public houses as their starting and finishing point. *Glover's History and Directory of Derby* for 1849 listed the following services:

> From the Rose and Crown in the Corn Market, a carrier service departed on three days a week for Alfreton, Ripley, Burton, Butterley, Chesterfield, Coxbench and Kilburn; on two days for Castle Donington, Hilton, Loughborough, Matlock and Shardlow; and once a week for Bradbourne, Breaston etc and Kegworth.
>
> From the Nag's Head in St Peter's Street on two days a week for Ashbourne, Milton and Repton; and once for Draycott, Etwall, Matlock, Marston and Sutton on the Hill.
>
> From the Queeen's Head in Victoria Street on three days a week for Ashby and Cromford; on two days for Castle Donington, Church Gresley, Hatton, Leicester etc., Shardlow, Swadlincote, Wirksworth and Wooden Box.
>
> From the Dolphin in Queen Street on six days per week for Heanor, Langley Mill, Shipley, Stanley and West Hallam; on three days for Duffield; and on one day for Brailsford, Codnor etc, Ilkeston, Morley, Sawley, Smalley and Stapleford.

At Chesterfield the Bird in the Hand, Cross Daggers, Crown and Cushion, Devonshire Arms, Old Angel, Old Star, Three Tuns and White Horse all provided a similar service. These inns made a vital contribution to the business life of the area, for it was here that parcels and letters could be collected and delivered, bills paid and fresh bookings made. It was not uncommon for the inn keeper to set aside a room for such business. As well as these local freight routes, many public houses and hotels also operated local horse-drawn omnibus services which existed to transport their patrons to and from the local railway station. This was particularly useful in Derby where the station lay on the edge of the town.

By the last quarter of the 19th century, theatres, music halls and dance halls were competing with the pub for customers. In Derby the Grand Theatre, which opened in 1886, offered the public variety shows, pantomime and touring productions. The Corn Exchange, later to become the Palace of Varieties, provided traditional music hall entertainment and the Lecture Theatre in the Wardwick attracted a number of celebrity speakers. But local pubs remained popular and many maintained an important social function. They were often still more comfortable than people's own homes and their largely male customers enjoyed not only beer but games of dominoes and cribbage.

They served as the meeting places of pigeon clubs, cycling clubs and football or cricket teams. Indeed, a number of local football teams began their lives as pub teams. The links with sporting teams was good business for the landlords of these pubs because in addition to any drinks they might sell they were often the venue for celebratory or 'end-of-season' suppers. In the 1890s at Crich several of the inter-village cricket matches ended with a supper at the Bulls Head; usually at a price of 1s 6d each. Some pubs had even closer links with local sporting clubs. The Wagon and Horses on Ashbourne Road, Derby, was the headquarters of the Derby and County Athletics Club and it was from here in March 1901 that the club launched a 10-mile championship race.

In the Peak District the growth of tourism and an increase in the popularity of healthy outdoor pursuits also had an impact on the services provided by local public houses. The growing popularity of visiting stately homes is reflected in an extract from Pigot's *Directory of Derbyshire* for 1835. Taking advantage of its proximity to Chatsworth House, the Devonshire Arms was described as being near to the Lodge and 'a house well conducted by Mr William Walters where every attention is paid to parties visiting this grand and romantic neighbourhood; from the inn is a pleasant road to Chatsworth house from which it is about a mile distant'. Elsewhere, the Old Park Hotel at Chapel en le Frith advertised 'good accommodation for cyclists' and 'every accommodation of picnic parties'. At spas such as Buxton and Matlock Bath, public houses and hotels provided for the needs of a diverse and wide-ranging clientele. It seems that the quality of the food and accommodation provided here had improved by the middle of the 19th century as Celia Feinnes, who visited Buxton in 1698, was scathing in her criticism. She complained that in addition to accommodation they were charged 'so much a piece for your dinners and suppers and so much for our servants besides'. The beer that was provided at meals, she said, was 'so bad that little can be drank' Her strongest criticism concerned the sleeping arrangements. Rooms were overcrowded and she commented that, 'if you have not company enough of your own to fill a room they will be ready to put others into the same chamber, and sometimes they are so crowded that three must lie in a bed'. Perhaps not surprisingly she reported that 'few people stay above two or three nights'.

Public houses also played an important role in national celebrations such as coronations and jubilees. In the case of King George III celebrations were also held to mark the King's return to health following bouts of madness. On 31 March 1790 a number of events were held in Derby. These included celebrations at the King's Head and the Bell Inn, where over 200 gentlemen sat down to a grand dinner at three o'clock in the afternoon. Many of them also attended a later event in the Market Place where a bonfire was lit and the Mayor and other representatives of the great and the good drank toasts to the King.

The Alma Inn public house at Melbourne.

Military victories were also a cause for celebration. In July 1813 the news reached Derby of the Duke of Wellington's victory at the Battle of Vitoria. On 5 July the Loyal Blue Club organised celebrations in the town. According to *The Derby Mercury*, church bells were rung and a sheep provided by them was roasted in the street. A sumptuous entertainment was laid on at the Mitre Tavern, where many toasts and sentiments were given including to the King, the Regent, the Queen and family, and Field Marshall Marquis Wellington.

Less than half a century later, the whole country was gripped by news of victory in the Crimean war. The Derbyshire Militia had distinguished itself in a number of engagements including the Battle of Alma, and it is not surprising that there was widespread rejoicing in Derby as well as other smaller towns. In Melbourne one of the public houses built around this time was named the Alma. It was some months before many of the troops returned home, but in January 1857 a dinner was given at the Anchor Inn, Bolsover, to mark the service of those who had served in the Crimean campaign. *The Derby Mercury* reported that 'The Sutton-in-Ashfield Glee Singers attended and contributed much to the harmony of the procedings'.

Public houses also joined in the celebrations to mark Queen Victoria's Golden Jubilee in 1887. *The Derby Mercury* reported that at Alfreton following a day of celebration a party of 70 sat down to an excellent dinner at the George and the evening concluded with a ball at the Angel. At Etwall, a series of meetings were held alternately at the two pubs in the village (the Hawk and Buckle and the Spread Eagle). Arising from these meetings, it was decided to arrange a two-course hot dinner plus a pint of ale for the men of the village and a tea for the women comprising two sorts of cake, bread and butter, buns and sandwiches.

The Alma Inn pub sign.

But times were changing and by the end of the Victorian era the more 'well-to-do' clientele of these establishments expected a high standard of accommodation. In 1899 the Angel Hotel in Chesterfield advised potential guests that it had been 'brought completely up to date in its arrangements and appliances'. The public rooms included a coffee room, commercial room and a fine billiard room containing three excellent billiard tables. The hotel provided 20 bedrooms, which were described as 'extremely comfortable and airy'. Many guests still arrived by horse and carriage and another feature of the hotel was the stabling, which provided accommodation for as many as 80 horses and a large number of vehicles.

The 19th century also saw growth in the number of commercial breweries and their associated 'tied houses'. By the middle of the century most towns in Derbyshire boasted at least one local brewery. These included Zachary Smith's Trent Brewery at Shardlow, Hill's of Cromford, Brunt, Bucknall & Co at Hartshorne and John Hair & Son at Melbourne. Chesterfield boasted three breweries and Derby four. Stretton's Derby Brewery was described in 1907 as 'by far the largest and most representative in the county' and including their interests in Loughborough and Birstall 'one of the largest enterprises in the Kingdom'. Before they were taken over in 1927 they supplied over 1,000 licensed houses spread over a large area in the Midlands and beyond.

The last independent brewer to survive in Derby was Offiler's. George Offiler began business in a small brewhouse at the rear of the Vine Inn at Derby in 1877, selling his surplus beer to other local pubs. Success led to expansion and in 1890 the brewery became a limited company with a share capital of £50,000. In the same year records show that the firm brewed 509,000 gallons of ale and owned 14 Derby pubs as well as 26 others scattered around Belper, South Derbyshire and Leicestershire. When the brewery was finally taken over in 1965 the company owned over 200 public houses.

But the growth in the consumption of alcohol caused concern in some quarters and the Victorian era also saw the growth of the temperance movement. Temperance hotels were established in some of the larger towns. Freeman's Temperance Commercial Hotel in Corporation Road, Chesterfield, was a typical example of such premises. Apart from being alcohol free, it provided all the comforts of similar licensed premises including 'handsomely furnished commercial and dining rooms, finely appointed billiard saloons, and 14 large, airy and comfortable bedrooms provided with every modern requisite and convenience, bathroom, lavatory etc'.

Illegal gambling was also a problem in some pubs. On 28 May 1880 Joseph Simnet, the landlord of the London Tavern on Hope Street, Derby, was arrested by the police for allowing gambling with cards in his pub. He was caught by a police constable going undercover disguised as an iron moulder, complete with a dirty face! When brought before the magistrates he was found guilty and was fined £10 with costs or two months' imprisonment. Similar cases were regularly reported in the local newspapers of the period. They were generally considered by the local police court and were dealt with by fines.

The 20th century saw a number of changes to the pub scene. In 1908 a General Children's Act contained provisions banning children under 14 altogether from the bars of licensed premises. The new law was not always obeyed and there are cases of mothers being prosecuted for sending their children into pubs to bring drinks home for them.

Licensing hours were reduced during World War One to ensure that a sober workforce was able to safely maintain high levels of production in munition factories. The same legislation was used to ban 'treating' so that the buying of rounds of drinks for friends was no longer permitted. The Defence of the Realm Act stipulated that 'All Licensed premises for the sale of intoxicating liquor within the area specified in the schedule shall be closed for the sale of intoxicating liquor to any persons not resident therein at 9 p.m.' This Act came into force in Derby on 5 January 1915 when Major J A Reeks signed a closing order which enforced the Act within a three-mile radius from Derby Market Place. A similar restriction was placed on a three-mile radius around Chesterfield, Baslow, Buxton and Swanwick. This legislation was generally unpopular and pub landlords complained that they were already paying higher taxes and that the same law did not apply to private clubs.

The war also had a considerable impact on local breweries. After only a few weeks Brampton Brewery had two of its lorries requisitioned and Stretton's Derby Brewery had most of its horses and all of its motor vehicles seized. They responded by placing a notice in the local newspaper which stated, 'We are glad to be of service to the State. We expect to be able to execute all orders entrusted to us. Should there be some delay during the next few days we crave the indulgence of our customers and hope quickly to be in a position to serve them as promptly as heretofore.'

As regiments were mobilised and more men recruited, Chesterfield began to resemble a garrison town. Most of the enlisted men were billeted in the drill hall but the officers found quarters at the Portland Hotel and other licensed houses. Elsewhere in the county the 2nd/6th Battalion of the Sherwood Foresters established a training camp at Buxton and commandeered the Empire Hotel as their headquarters.

Plans were made to cope with the large numbers of expected casualties. Special hospitals for Canadian servicemen were established at Peak Hydro in Buxton and the Royal Hotel in Matlock Bath. The Palace Hotel and the Empire Hotel (also in Buxton) were both used as an annexe of the Granville Military Hospital.

One result of increased regulation was a dramatic decline in cases of drunkenness. The Defence of the Realm legislation was strictly enforced and throughout the war a number of landlords found themselves in court for breaching these orders. In October 1915 Frank Eyre, the landlord of the Windmill pub in Derby, was fined £5 for permitting drunkenness on his premises. Others found themselves in trouble for selling intoxicating liquor beyond the permitted hours. In 1916 Arthur White, the licensee of the Castle Fields pub on Siddals Road, Derby, was fined £5 plus costs for selling intoxicating liquor at 10.25pm. After a second offence a closing order was made by the military authorities and the pub never reopened! Profiteering by selling beer above the fixed price was also prohibited during the war and on 30 August 1918 Walter Buxton, the licensee of the Harrow Inn at Ilkeston, was convicted of selling a pint of beer for 6d (50 per cent above the legal limit of 4d). Similar convictions were reported against the landlords of the Prince of Wales in Ilkeston, the Red Lion at Matlock Green and Hodgkinson's Hotel in Matlock Bath.

World War Two also had a significant impact on public houses. As early as September 1939 an advance party of the 2nd (North Midland) Signals Corps arrived in Bakewell and established an officers' mess at the Rutland Arms Hotel. Some pubs, particularly in rural areas, were also used by the Home Guard for meetings or training. The Hayfield Company met each week at the George Inn. At Birchover, the landlord of the Druid Inn was a member of the Home Guard and often tucked a bottle of whisky inside his tunic. It is said that on a cold night his comrades always kept close to him!

As the war progressed some pubs benefitted from the construction of RAF airfields and temporary army camps. The George and Dragon in the Market Place at Ashbourne became a popular watering hole for servicemen and women stationed at the nearby airfield, whereas soldiers based at Hardwick Hall made their way to the pubs in Chesterfield on a Saturday night. In 1942 the first American servicemen began to arrive in Derby. The US forces adopted a strict policy of racial segregation and different nights were prescribed for black and white soldiers to travel into the town to visit its pubs.

For the civilian population the pub was described as 'a blockhouse on the home front' and praised for its contribution to maintaining the morale of the nation. Derbyshire suffered little from German bombing but one Member of Parliament described the pub as 'the one place where after dark the collective heart of the race could be seen and felt, beating resolute and strong'. In Derbyshire, as elsewhere in the country, pubs raised considerable amounts of money for the war effort by a variety of means. Collection boxes on the bar raised money for campaigns such as 'Spitfire Week' and the 'Derby and District Fighter Plane Fund'.

An indirect consequence of the war was a growth in the number of women frequenting pubs. Increased social and financial independence coupled with an uncertain future led to more and more women beginning to spend some of their free time in local hostelries. They were able to let their hair down and relax from the burden of war work and the emotional stress caused by the conflict. It also provided an opportunity to meet members of the opposite sex. A good number of marriages were launched in the bars of Derbyshire pubs!

Rationing and the disruption of manufacturing and trade in World War Two led to a shortage of both beer and glasses. The strength of beer was also reduced. Older members of the community recall sometimes having to use jam jars to drink their beer! There were even shortages of beer to celebrate VJ Day. At Belper it was reported that the pubs closed early as they had sold out of beer the previous weekend!

The post-war period also saw a number of significant developments in the licensed trade. Pubs had benefitted during the war from an increase in the number of women visiting their premises and they set out to retain that custom. Many pubs were 'smartened up', a wider range of drinks was now on offer and meals became more generally available.

In the 1960s and 70s new estate pubs were built to serve the growing suburbs of Derby and Chesterfield. These were often bland and uninteresting buildings with equally bland and unexciting names such as the Robin at Mickleover, the Kingfisher at Chaddesden and the Oak and Acorn at Oakwood. There were a few exceptions. The Honeycomb on the Silverhill Estate in Mickleover was designed around an unusual octagonal design which was reflected in its name. Also in Mickleover, in the 1970s a

Pullman Coach was attached to the Nags Head to provide an unusual restaurant.

The 60s also saw a revival in the demand for real ale and CAMRA (the Campaign for Real Ale) was founded. Today the Derby Branch is flourishing with its own magazine and regular beer festivals. It also has its own system of awards for such things as City Pub of the Year and County Pub of the Year. This growth in the popularity of real ale also led to the development of micro-breweries, often based in pubs. The first of these in Derbyshire was at the John Thomson Inn at Ingleby, where the first pint of JTS XXX was pulled in 1977 to celebrate the Queen's

The Flower Pot is a popular venue for live music.

Silver Jubilee. During the last few years there has been a huge increase both locally and nationally in the number of micro- breweries and some of these have established their own small chains of public houses. A good example is the Derby Brewery Company which now owns the Greyhound and the Tap, both in Derby, as well as the Queens Head at Little Eaton and the Kedleston Country House Hotel.

This period also saw a revival of the pub as a place of entertainment, with folk and jazz clubs being a popular feature at many. Many of these remain important venues for live music. One of the best known is the Flower Pot in Derby, which has hosted a number of star names over the years, including Nils Lofgren, Glenn Tilbrook, Midge Ure, Beverley Craven, Squeeze and Nine Below Zero. The venue has also become renowned for attracting top-notch blues bands and some of the world's best tribute acts.

Many pubs hosted not only darts teams but also sponsored angling, football and cricket clubs. And bingo, karaoke and quizzes became features of the weekly round. In the countryside many pubs closed down as a consequence of the drink-driving laws or turned themselves into restaurants or gastro-pubs where the drinker sometimes felt driven out. In towns, some have been converted into convenience stores. In Derby the Blue Pool at Sunnyhill and the Blue Boy in Chaddesden are good examples of

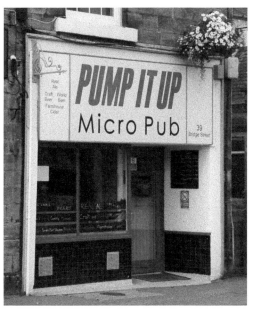

The Pump It Up micro-pub in Belper.

this trend. The Derbyshire Yeoman near Markeaton Park road island closed in 1991 and reopened shortly afterwards as a drive-thru McDonald's fast food outlet. Some pubs have been converted into private residences, others have been demolished to make way for housing or other uses. The Victoria in Cowley Street, which used to attract students as well as local residents, is now student accommodation for the University of Derby.

The 21st century has seen a number of trends emerging including the growth in popularity of craft beers and the emergence of the micro pub. These are very small, often one room, public houses which are defined by the Micro-pub Association as 'a small free house which listens to its customers, mainly serves cask ales, promotes conversation, shuns all forms of electronic entertainment and dabbles in traditional pub snacks'. Such pubs have grown in number in Derbyshire during the last few years and include the Chip and Pin in Melbourne, The Little Chester Ale House in Derby and Pump it Up in Belper. So, from mansiones to micro-pubs the people of Derbyshire have enjoyed a visit to their 'local' for almost 2,000 years!

PUBS WITH A PAST

Some of the oldest pubs in the county were demolished in the second half of the 20th century. In Derby these included the Old Angel, the Nottingham Castle and the Horse and Trumpet. In recent years others have been converted to a different use. But this is not a one-way street. The Wetherspoons pub chain has converted a number of historic buildings into public houses and the recent trend towards the opening of micro-pubs has seen banks, post offices, shops and even private houses all converted into pubs These have included the Last Post at the Rowditch in Derby and the Chip and Pin at Melbourne.

Despite these changes there remain many pubs in the county with an interesting past. The following are just a few examples of Derbyshire's rich public-house history and heritage.

The Bell Inn at Sadlergate, Derby, was built around 1680 and was for many years one of the principal coaching inns of the town. Stage coaches with names such as the Telegraph, the Lady Nelson, the Defiance and the Champion provided regular services to London, Manchester, Leeds, Nottingham and elsewhere in the kingdom. The Bell was also used for a variety of social, civic, business and judicial functions. Inquests and courts were held here and the inn also played host to doctors, vets and other professional men who plied their trades from here. The Bell also played its part in national rejoicing. In March 1790 the King's recovery from an attack of lunacy was celebrated with a formal dinner. Tickets were seven-and-sixpence each, with a ball for the ladies at five shillings. In September 1831 a public dinner was held here to celebrate the coronation of King William IV and Queen Adelaide. *The Derby Mercury* reported that the Mayor presided, and that 'about forty gentlemen sat down to an excellent dinner, well served' with 'very superior' wines. A number of tradesmen's organisations held their meetings at the Bell. In December 1784 *The Derby Mercury* reported that at a 'very numerous and respectable meeting of the tradesmen of the town' it was 'unanimously agreed and resolved to abolish the giving of Christmas Boxes to their customers, having followed the example of several capital towns'. To prevent any 'backsliding' an article was entered into, subjecting every person to a 'considerable penalty who shall break through or evade such agreement'. In the 1770s the Bell was purchased by the Campion family, who ran it for just over a century, adding a fine ballroom at the rear. Viscount Torrington visited in 1790 and was not impressed. He complained that the inn was 'only served by females who run around like rabbits; and five of who are not the equal of one man waiter'. The landlord he described as 'fat, stupid and splay-footed'. The Bell continued

The Bell Inn, Derby.

as a coaching inn until 1855 when the last coach departed. In 1928 it was bought by the St James' Hotel Company and rebuilt. The work was carried out by local contractors Ford & Weston, who created a 'mock-Tudor' facade. As part of the remodelling they created a Tudor Room using architectural salvage. For many years this was the haunt of the great and the good in Derby, including businessmen, councillors and journalists.

In 1989 the building was threatened with plans to convert it to shop units but was saved on conservation grounds. During the remaining years of the 20th century the Bell suffered mixed fortunes. It was closed in 2012 after a fatal stabbing on the street just outside. In 2013 the Bell was purchased by a local businessman who invested £1m in restoring the inn to its former glory. It reopened in July 2015.

The Bell Inn at Cromford was one of two pubs that once stood on either side of North Street at its junction with Cromford Hill (the Cock Inn being the other). Richard Arkwright built North Street in 1776-77 to house his mill workers, although the pub was not opened

The Bell Inn pub sign.

until a few years later. The earliest known landlord (1828) was James Gell. He was also a maltster and it is possible that he brewed beer on the premises. In the 19th century the pub was popular with the mill workers and other workmen who lived or worked in the area. In January 1880 *The Derby Mercury* of 21 January reported that on the previous Saturday the workmen employed on the High Peak Railway (Cromford and Hopton Section) had their annual supper at the Bell Inn. Upwards of 50 people sat down to the well-furnished tables to enjoy the excellent and

The Bell Inn, Cromford.

substantial fare provided by the host, Mr Mee. After a number of speeches, an enjoyable evening was spent, the musical members of the company contributing greatly towards the general enjoyment! The pub has continued to serve the local community to the present day and remains popular with locals and visitors alike.

The Blackmoor's Head at Ashbourne dates from at least the early years of the 18th century. Like the neighbouring Green Man, it was for many years a successful coaching inn. As one of the principal inns of the town, the Blackmoor's Head was used to conduct a wide range of important business. This included inquisitions, courts, archdeacon's visitations and in 1748 even the county assizes were held there. During the Napoleonic Wars, French prisoners of war were billeted there. Some of these were members of the French nobility and it is said that one of the rooms was used by a French priest to celebrate a Catholic mass for his fellow countrymen. Following a decline in the coaching trade the Blackmoor's Head was purchased by the owner of the Green Man in 1825.

The Bluebell Inn at Tissington dates from the 16th century but remained a working farm until 1984. For many years it was a stopping place for coaches and drovers who traversed the area.

The Bridge Inn at Duffield was built on the site of the former Bull's Head pub. It was renamed as the Bridge Inn in 1815 and was sold by auction at the White Hart along with other properties in the village. A number of landlords had problems in conducting the business and a variety of incidents were reported in the local press. In 1857 William Lynam accidentally killed himself with a gun following an argument with his customers. A few years later, in 1862, George Knifton pleaded guilty to 'having permitted drunk and disorderly conduct in his house'. In 1896 Samuel Kirk,

The Bridge Inn, Duffield.

who was described as being both an innkeeper and farmer, pleaded guilty to being drunk on his own premises. He was fined 10s with 9s 6d costs. In a separate case he was charged with an aggravated assault on his wife, but the case was dropped as he was considered to be 'a good father and husband if only he would leave the drink alone'. Another landlord had a more positive impact on the community. In 1900 John Bancroft organised a fishing match on the River Derwent and offered a prize for the heaviest catch of the day. In the following year he saved Miss Ada Suggatt from drowning and was recognised for his bravery by the Royal Humane Society. Inquests were held here, and in 1904 *The Derby Daily Telegraph* reported on the enquiry into the death of a man found drowned in the river. In 1936 the existing inn was demolished and replaced with the present building. *The Derby Daily Telegraph* reported that 'The Bridge Inn at Duffield, once a favourite resort of anglers ... is now being demolished. The inn, however, will not disappear for on the old site a modern building is being erected in which many of the features of the old house will be retained'. In order to allow the business to continue without interruption, it was reported that 'part of the new building has already been erected while the demolition of the old building is proceeding as rapidly as possible'. During the 1940s the pub supported both the war effort and a variety of local good causes. In January 1941 it donated £2 5s 8d to the Derby and District Fighter Plane Fund and in April 1943 the pub raised £100 for the

Duffield Wings for Victory Campaign by auctioning a barrel of beer. For a number of years an annual show of flowers and vegetables was held here in aid of the Derbyshire Royal Infirmary. The Bridge Inn still plays an important part in the social life of the local community. Local football teams and a fishing club meet here and a quiz takes place on Thursday and Sunday evenings.

The Broadway Hotel near Darley Park was built in the 1840s as a private house, known first as Tresilian and later as Darley Lodge. In 1933 the then owner, William Haddon Williams, sold the house which was opened as the Broadway and subsequently altered and extended. The licence was transferred from the Wheatsheaf in Walker Lane by Stretton's Brewery. The granting of a licence to the Broadway Hotel was opposed by the Derby Temperance Federation and about 150 local residents. These objections were rejected by the magistrates, who declared that providing a licence for the new hotel was 'altogether to the benefit of the people of the district and a credit to all concerned'. The Broadway has changed ownership a number of times over the past 80 years or so. It is now part of the Hungry Horse chain.

The Brunswick Inn at Derby is believed to have been the first-ever specifically-built railway inn and was originally known as the Brunswick Railway and Commercial Inn. It was built by the Midland Railway Company in a development which also included 90 houses for railway employees and four shops. The Brunswick was typical of the urban public house of the Victorian era. It comprised a tap room (bar), smoke room (saloon) and parlour (best room). It also had a small private bar or snug which could be used by private groups or sometimes by women only. The Brunswick Inn brewed its own ale in a brewhouse in the adjacent yard. The beer was served by pot boys from a central location. The inn opened in June 1842 and from the outset it catered for employees of the Midland Railway and the nearby locomotive and carriage and wagon works. It also provided accommodation for the growing band of commercial travellers who used the railways to ply their trade. In December 1850 a small group of Midland Railway employees met here and agreed to form a Reading Society. A notice in a local newspaper shortly after the opening of the inn advertised the following terms:

Breakfast, plain	1s 6d
Ditto, with Meat etc	2s 0d
Dinner	2s 0d
Tea	1s 6d
Supper	1s 6d
Beds	2s 0d
Wine	5s per bottle

It remained in railway ownership for 105 years before being taken over by Hardy and Hanson Brewery in 1947. It closed in the 1960s when the Borough Council proposed to demolish the area in order to extend the inner ring road. This scheme was rejected and the Brunswick Inn re-opened in 1987, following restoration on behalf of the Derby Civic Society and the Derbyshire Historic Buildings Trust. Four years later the then owner, Trevor Harris, established a brewery on the premises. The pub has won several awards and in 2001 was voted UK Beer Pub of the Year.

The Brunswick Inn.

The Bull's Head at Hartshorne dates in part from around 1600, although the Georgian style frontage is early 19th century. It is a substantial building and a notice of sale in 1846 described it as having an adjoining bake house and stabling for 12 horses. As the principal inn of the area, it provided accommodation for a number of

The Bull's Head, Hartshorne.

business, social and official functions. Sales of land and property took place there and the trustees of the Moira and Gresley turnpikes regularly met at the Bull's Head. William Raven was the owner and landlord from the early years of the 18th century. When he died in 1755 his son Gilbert took on the running of the pub on behalf of his mother. The Bull's Head was a substantial property and Gilbert himself was a man of some wealth and importance in the community. During the mid-1760s the Enclosure Commissioners held their deliberations at the Bull's Head, where they divided up and reallocated the open fields and common land in the area. Gilbert himself acquired 33 acres of land from the subsequent Enclosure Act. In common with other pubs, inquests were held here during this period. As this was a mining area, many of these were related to colliery accidents. In June 1869 an enquiry was held into the death of Thomas Thacker who worked at the nearby Granville Colliery. A lump of coal had fallen on him and he suffered a fractured skull. The surgeon, Mr Croft, gave evidence that he had removed about half an ounce of coal from the deceased brain. A verdict of accidental death was returned. Today the Bull's Head operates as a free house with a good local reputation for food. It also attracts visitors to the area with a number of comfortable en-suite rooms

The Bull's Head at Repton dates from the 18th century and was at one time a posting inn with its own stables. For almost two centuries it played an important role in the social and business life of the village. Sales of land, property and other items took place at the Bull's Head and a number of organisations hosted their meetings here. These included the Repton Society for the Prosecution of Felons and an organisation called the Order of Free Gardeners. This was a fraternal society with some similarity to freemasonry. Like numerous other friendly societies of the time, its principal aim was the sharing of secret knowledge linked to the profession and mutual aid. *The Derby Mercury* of 28 June 1846 reported the founding of the Repton Lodge in following manner:

> ORDER OF ANCIENT FREE GARDENERS
> On Monday week a Lodge of the above Order was opened at the house of Mr Marshall, Bulls Head Inn, Repton when 52 persons were initiated into the mysteries of Free Gardening. After the business was over the party sat down to an excellent supper…the usual loyal and other toasts were drunk and the evening was spent in mirth and harmony. On the following day the wives of the new members to the number of 68 were regaled with tea &c. The evening was occupied with dancing.

A number of meetings were held at the Bull's Head to conduct local business. Tenants paid their rents to Sir Francis Burdett, the local squire, and usually enjoyed a dinner here after the business was concluded. These tenants must have been particularly grateful to the squire in 1881 for *The Derby Mercury* reported that at his half-yearly rent audit 'Sir Francis Burdett Bart. returned 13% on their rents for the half year to all his tenants on the Foremark Estate'. A number of social events including formal dinners were held at the Bull's Head but not all passed without incident. In July 1898 William Hill, a labourer from Willington, appeared in the local Police Court where he admitted to refusing to quit the Bull's Head when requested to do so. It seems that the man caused numerous disturbances in the pub and as a consequence the landlord refused to serve him. It was reported that 'while a big dinner was taking place the defendant made himself very obnoxious and had to be ejected five or six times'. In mitigation the defendant said that he was very drunk and would not do such a thing again. He was fined 2s 6d and 12s 6d costs. The Bull's Head continued to be a popular local venue for much of the 20th century but later fell into disrepair. It was extensively renovated and is today a highly successful gastro-pub and restaurant.

The Carpenters Arms at Dale Abbey was built in 1880 by the Hollingworths. They were a well-established local family who had previously owned the Blue Bell in the village. It seems that the Carpenters Arms was an extension of an earlier structure as parts of the pub date back to the 17th century. It was extended again in the 19th

The Carpenters Arms at Dale Abbey.

century and the front of the pub dates from this period. Over the years it has played a significant part in the life of the village. Sales of land, property, livestock, furniture and other items took place here. It was also a venue for cock fighting. Local residents also remember tales being told of haymaking when youngsters would be sent to the Carpenters Arms to fetch beer in one-gallon stone jars to refresh the thirsty haymakers. For a number of years the Dale Abbey Association for the Prosecution of Felons held their meetings here. In common with pubs elsewhere at this time, inquests were held here. These were often unremarkable, but in December 1892 the local press reported an inquest into 'the mysterious death of a West Hallam Schoolmistress'. It appears that Annie Mary Cliff, a single woman and for five years assistant mistress at West Hallam Schools, died as a consequence of a botched abortion which may have been conducted in Nottingham. The verdict was one of wilful murder against some person or persons unknown. The latter years of the 19th century also saw an increase in the local organisation of political parties. In February 1892 *The Derbyshire Times and Chesterfield Herald* reported that the local Conservative Association held a well-attended smoking concert at the Carpenters Arms. As a village pub, it is not surprising that the Carpenters Arms was involved in country pursuits, and in the 1930s the Earl of Harrington's Hunt met here on a number of occasions. Little is known about the pub in the years that followed and it features infrequently in newspaper reports. The village remains largely unchanged and only a few new houses have been built. The growth in private car ownership has probably increased custom, although the pub today also benefits from walkers, cyclists and even horse riders who call into the pub for food and refreshments.

The Cheshire Cheese at Buxton dates from around 1787. It provided food and lodging for a wide range of visitors, including actors performing at the theatre. One of these, the actor S W Ryley, recalled having enjoyed a 'fine trout supper' there. The hotel attracted a more middle-class clientele than the establishments nearer the Crescent. In common with other hostelries in Buxton, the Cheshire Cheese operated as a coaching inn for the regular London to Manchester service. By 1835 it was listed as a carrier's inn. It has been suggested that this implied its trade came more from the working classes than those hostelries nearer the Crescent. Whatever the truth, by 1855 the inn had its own bowling green which was advertised as the only one in Buxton. The landlord promised that it would be, 'kept in good condition for the lovers of that fine old English manly game'. The Cheshire Cheese continued to cater for the needs of tourists. In 1880 the landlord advertised that he had 'a handsome omnibus well adapted for parties to Chatsworth and other places of interest in the neighbourhood'. The exterior of the hotel has changed little since the 18th century but has adapted to serve the needs of its present-day customers. Home cooked food is served daily and entertainment includes live music and a weekly quiz.

The Clock Warehouse, Shardlow.

The Clock Warehouse at Shardlow was built as a canal warehouse in the 18th century. Straddling an arm of the Trent and Mersey Canal, narrow boats were able to sail beneath a central arch and load and unload goods directly in to the floors above. For over 100 years the village was an important transhipment point between the Trent and Mersey Canal and the River Trent and was known as 'a rural Rotterdam' and a 'Little Liverpool'. Following the demise of the canal, the building lay derelict for a number of years but in 1975 the village was declared a conservation area. A number of buildings were renovated and the clock warehouse became a heritage centre celebrating the canal era. When this closed the building was converted to a pub (Hoskin's Wharf) and is today known as the Clock Warehouse.

The Coopers Arms at Weston on Trent was originally a private residence known as Weston Hall. Construction was started in 1663 but for a variety of reasons was never completed as planned. The area was affected by the Civil War and according to legend Sir John Gell used the hall as a barracks, stabling 200 horses in the under-croft. Over the centuries ownership of the house changed several times before passing into the hands of the Cooper family in 1942. It was in a partly ruinous state and it is said that for a number of years the basement area was used to grow forced rhubarb. Extensive structural renovations took place in the 1970s, and in 1989 Tom Cooper and his wife decided to transform the hall into a public house and restaurant. It opened as the Coopers Arms in 1991. Many of the original features were retained including oak panelling and an enormous stone fireplace with side ovens.

The Crispin Inn at Ashover has a fascinating history. According to local legend the inn probably dates from 1416 when Thomas Babington of Dethick and several men of Asher (presumably archers) returned from the Battle of Agincourt which was fought on Saint Crispin's Day. A more likely explanation is that the inn, which was once occupied by a cobbler, was named after Saint Crispin, who was patron saint of cobblers, tanners and leather workers. During the English Civil

The Coopers Arms, Weston on Trent.

The Crispin Inn, Ashover.

War, the area was the scene of fighting between Royalist and Roundhead soldiers. According to a sign outside the inn: 'In 1646 Job Wall, the landlord of the Crispin Inn withstood the King's Troops in the doorway and told them they should have no more drink in his house as they had had too much already. But they turned him out and sat watch at the door until all the ale was drunk or wasted'.

The Crown Inn at Allenton was built in 1891 at a cost of £1,200. In April 1895 workmen digging a well on the premises discovered the ossified remains of a hippopotamus. The remains are believed to date back 120,000 years when the area was covered by a tropical swamp. The excavation of the bones was funded by a group of local worthies who agreed that they should be donated to Derby Museum. They remain there today and still generate a great deal of interest. The discovery of the hippopotamus was commemorated in 1995 when a plaque was unveiled at the pub marking the centenary of its original discovery.

The Dog and Duck at Shardlow is thought to be the oldest pub in the village and was built close to what was then the centre of the village. It is thought that the annual wakes were held nearby and this no doubt brought increased custom to the pub. Not a great deal is known about its early history, but during the 19th century it fulfilled the functions of a typical village pub with various local organisations holding their meetings there. The Loyal Cavendish Lodge of Oddfellows and the Female Friendly

The Dog and Duck, Shardlow.

Society both met at the Dog and Duck; and in November 1896 *The Derby Mercury* reported that a half-yearly rent audit was held there for the tenants of Rev Roby Burgin. A good dinner was provided, consisting of 'roast beef and pork and a good supply of vegetables, pastry and the usual dainties'. The announcement that landlord, the Rev. Burgin, would make a reduction of 10 per cent was warmly received and his health was drunk with great enthusiasm. The pub did not always enjoy such peace and harmony. A few years earlier, in September 1881, the landlord had occasion to turn two men out for 'larking'. According to a report in *The Derby Daily Telegraph* one of them, David Clayton, stood at the door with a big stick and when asked what he was going to do with it he replied, 'I am going to strike you'. He then flew at the landlord and assaulted him so severely that he was knocked down and blood flowed from the wounds inflicted. The magistrates found him guilty of assault and fined him £3 and costs or in default one month's imprisonment. The pub continued to contribute to the social life of the village in the first half of the 20th century. The local cricket and angling clubs held their meetings and annual dinners here and the pub also hosted carnation and gooseberry shows. In the 1920s and 1930s the pub had an outing club which arranged visits to the seaside and other places of interest. They seemed to pack a lot into a day, for in 1930 after an early start they travelled to Cleethorpes and, following lunch, went on to Sutton and Mablethorpe. Returning to Sutton for tea, they stopped at Lincoln to see the Cathedral and Newark to visit the castle. According to a local newspaper account, 'after a very enjoyable day favoured by splendid weather the party arrived back shortly after ten o'clock'. Over the past few decades the pub has undergone a number of changes in ownership. It suffered a devastating fire in 2011 and was closed for some time. It is at present a Marston's eatery-style pub which attracts a loyal clientele.

The Dog and Partridge lies on Swinscoe Hill just outside Ashbourne. It dates from the early 17th century. John Byng stayed here in 1789. He described it as a poor alehouse where he 'ate and drank furiously of some soft bad oaten cakes, cheese and ale'. A serious accident involving the London to Manchester coach known as the Telegraph occurred just outside the pub on New Year's Day 1830. *The Staffordshire Advertiser* reported that 'The coachman was accidentally thrown off his box and pulled a passenger down with him. The horses experiencing liberty, went down the hill at full speed, crossed the bridge at the bottom, and carried the coach with great violence against the public house on the opposite side, forcing off one of the wheels. They then galloped towards the toll bar where the coach came into contact with the gate-post and was dashed almost to pieces.' The pub has changed little since this time. It has been owned by the same family for over 20 years and is a popular base for visitors to the Peak District.

The Dolphin Inn, Derby.

The Dolphin Inn in Queen Street, Derby, dates back to 1530 and is believed to be Derby's oldest pub. In the first half of the 19th century, it was the starting point for a number of local carrier services to destinations such as Duffield. Eastwood, Heanor, Ilkeston and West Hallam. The Dolphin was always a large and impressive inn. A notice in *The Derby Mercury* on 1 August 1872 described it as having an 'important frontage of 43ft 9in to Queen Street' as well as 'most excellent cellars'. It also contained 'tap room, bar-parlour, large dining room and four bed rooms and attics, kitchen, store room and other conveniences'. In addition, there was a brewhouse in the yard and stabling for 12 horses. With such facilities it is not surprising that the Dolphin played host to a number of local organisations and was used to celebrate great local and national events. In March 1863 celebrations were held throughout the town to mark the marriage of the Prince of Wales. Among the festivities of the day, worthy of record was that of a substantial hot luncheon at the Dolphin Inn provided by Mr Hefford (a local industrialist) to all his workers. A few years later, in August 1877, *The Derby Mercury* reported that 'the Female Friendly Society celebrated their anniversary at the Dolphin Inn by tea &c and a friendly dance'. With a location close to the centre of the town, it is not surprising that the Dolphin was sometimes the scene of drunkenness and minor crime. Minor infringements of the licensing laws were presented to the Police Court, as were incidents of customers being drunk and disorderly. In the 1920s the

The Eagle Hotel, Buxton.

Dolphin also operated as a 'wine store'. A notice in *The Derby Daily Telegraph* of 20 December 1927 headed 'Wines For Christmas' advised readers that the landlord had for sale his 'noted Douro Port', which he was able to supply for 2/6 per bottle. The same advertisement declared that every known brand of wines, spirits and liquors were in stock at 'popular prices'. The Dolphin claims to be the most haunted pub in Derby and is a regular calling place on 'ghost walks' It is also a popular live music and quiz venue and is listed on the Campaign for Real Ale's National Inventory of Historic Pub Interiors.

The Eagle Hotel in Buxton was originally known as the Eagle and Child and was first recorded in 1592. The original building was purchased by the 3rd Duke of Devonshire in 1746 and rebuilt by the 5th Duke in 1760. Further extensions were made between 1780 and 1790 to cater for the coaching trade. There was fierce rivalry between different hostelries for the custom provided by these coaches and an agreement was made between the Eagle and the White Hart. Passengers travelling South to London ate at the White Hart, while those travelling North to Manchester dined at the Eagle. Following the demise of the coaching trade half of the building was converted into a lodging house, but within a few years business had recovered and it

The Falcon Inn, Chesterfield.

was reincorporated back into the Eagle Hotel. In the second half of the 19th century the hotel was used to host town meetings. These were presided over by the Duke's agent and tenants were encouraged to raise concerns, consider problems and make suggestions for improvements to the town. For a brief period during the Edwardian era the hotel changed its name to the Devonshire Hotel. This may have been an attempt to attract a more upmarket clientele, but it was unsuccessful and it soon reverted to its original name.

The Falcon Inn at Chesterfield is today a branch of the Yorkshire Building Society. The building dates from the 16th century. Little is known about its early history although, despite popular belief, there is no evidence that it was ever a coaching inn. In the early years of the 19th century, Chesterfield provided accommodation for French prisoners of war and some were billeted at the Falcon Inn. One of these, Colonel Richemont, was the victim of a serious robbery. According to *The Star* newspaper of 1807, £1,500 was stolen from his strong box while he was lodging at the inn. The thief was found to be one of his comrades, who committed suicide before he could be brought to trial. Local newspapers also provide evidence of the business carried on in the inn. It was commonplace for a pub landlord to carry on a second occupation. In 1852, Mr Smith, the landlord, was recorded as being the owner of a coal pit near Brimington. Land and property were auctioned here as well as turnpike tolls. The Chesterfield Association for the Prosecution of Felons met at the Falcon, and in 1892 a special meeting of the Derbyshire Miners' Association was convened at the Falcon to consider a number of matters, including the provision of support to striking miners in other parts of the country. Only a few years later the building changed ownership and became the Everest Dining Rooms for almost a century. It was next purchased by the Barnsley Building Society. This in turn was taken over by the Yorkshire Building Society. It remains today an interesting feature of the Chesterfield townscape.

The Gate Inn at Stanton in South Derbyshire was built sometime in the 1820s when it was known as the Park Gate. By the 1870s the pub was also recorded as a tollgate, and the landlord, Joseph Redfern, was listed as the tollgate keeper. Some idea of the size of this inn can be gleaned from a notice of sale which appeared in *The Burton Chronicle* on 23 July 1891. The property was described as a 'fully licensed Free House with Dairy, Stabling, Piggeries, other out buildings and good-sized garden'. The same notice also listed 'Taproom, Parlour, Houseplace, Kitchen, Pantry, Cellar, Washhouse, 4 bedrooms and the usual out offices'. In addition, nine acres of land consisting of three pastures were also offered for sale. For a number of years during the 19th century the field at the rear of the inn was the site of the annual Stanton Wakes Week, when various amusements and fairground stalls were erected there. This was a popular event which brought additional custom but a Top Up Supper was also held at the end of the week when the food was provided by the landlady of the Gate Inn. The original pub sign took the form of a small wooden gate on which was painted the following words: 'This Gate hangs well and hinders none, Refresh and pay and travel on'. This was replaced in 1993 when a more modern sign took its place.

The George Hotel at Hathersage is believed to have been built at some time in the 16th century, although some sources place it as earlier. It provided accommodation for travellers and served the packhorse trains that wound their way from Sheffield and Castleton. Charlotte Bronte visited whilst writing her novel *Jane Eyre*. Hathersage provided the inspiration for the village of Morton which she named after the landlord of the George Inn.

The George Inn on Irongate, Derby, (now **Jorrocks**) was one of Derby's principal coaching inns. The first coach service to London was inaugurated from here in 1735. It ran once a week, taking three or four days to complete the journey in good weather! The London to Nottingham stage coach ran from the George from 1775, and in 1776

Jorrocks, previously the George, Derby.

the Post Office coach also departed from here. The yard at the rear of the inn was once used for cock fighting and a balconied extension was built so that the customers could watch such contests as well as other forms of entertainment. In 1745 the George became the headquarters of the Duke of Devonshire, where he raised the Derbyshire Blues to combat the invading army of Prince Charles Edward Stuart (Bonnie Prince Charlie). The troops were withdrawn before the arrival of the highland army and it was

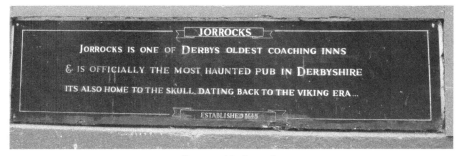

Sign outside Jorrocks.

to the George that the advance guard of the Prince's army arrived on 4 December 1745 to demand billets for 9,000 men. Throughout the 18th and 19th centuries the George hosted a number of important social functions and celebratory dinners. Despite this, Viscount Torrington who visited in 1789 wrote that 'the George Inn stands awkwardly and is one of those dark, narrow, noisy town inns that abominate'. In the same year *The Derby Mercury* reported that Thomas Mather, having been sworn in as Mayor, 'gave a sumptuous entertainment at the George Inn to the gentlemen of the Corporation and many other town and country gentlemen'. The dinner consisted of 'almost every rarity that the season could produce'. According to the same report, 'many joyous songs were sung, and the day was spent in the most convivial manner'. In the first half of the 19th century, half of the inn was divided into shop fronts and much reduced in size. During the 20th century the George changed its name a number of times and was known variously as Mr Jorrocks, Lafferty's and the Globe Vaults. It remains a popular city centre pub but little remains to indicate its long history.

The George Hotel in Tideswell was built in 1730 and was once a coaching inn. John Byng stayed here in 1790. He described it as a comfortable public house where he was 'instantly served with cold roast beef and cold pigeon pie'. His total bill came to two shillings and sixpence, which included 10 pence for food and one shilling and sixpence for wine. He was charged five pence for hay and corn for his horse. The exterior of the hotel remains very much as it was 300 years ago. It describes itself today as a family-run inn with traditional pub food and rooms.

The Green Man in Ashbourne was built in the middle of the 18th century to serve the growing coach trade in the town. For many years it played an important role in the social life of the town, although in many ways it was less important than the Blackmoor's Head. Nevertheless, dances, balls and celebratory dinners were held here. In April 1789 a dinner was held to commemorate the King's restoration to health. Sir William Fitzherbert from Tissington Hall took the chair, and the stewards were Richard Beresford, John Alsopp and John Port (all members of wealthy and influential local families). In 1809 the King's 50th Jubilee was celebrated at both the Green Man and the Blackmoor's Head with balls which were numerously attended at both establishments. Dancing masters regularly visited Ashbourne, usually holding their classes at the Green Man. These classes were often followed by balls at which the young students of these dancing masters could demonstrate their elegance and deportment. By the early years of the 19th century, the importance of Ashbourne as a social centre was beginning to wane. This decline was highlighted in 1825 when the proprietor of the Green Man bought out his long-standing rival, the Blackmoor's Head, closed it down and amalgamated it with his own business. In the 1830s Princess (later Queen) Victoria, stopped here briefly during her tour of Britain, and the owner later changed the name to 'The Green Man and Black's Head Royal Hotel'. Subsequently, the addition of 'Commercial' allowed the owners to claim that it was the longest inn name in Britain. The coming of the railways put an end to the lucrative coaching trade. By 1846 there was only one coach passing through the town, and by 1855 the coaching trade has ceased entirely. The Green Man continued to play an important role in the social and commercial life of the town. Sales and auctions were regularly held here and, as one of the most substantial licensed houses in the town, the Green Man continued to host a number of dinners and other social functions. From the latter years of the 19th century, the Green Man began to rely more on the tourist trade. A notice in *The Derbyshire Advertiser and Journal* in 1896 advertised 'Splendid accommodation for Tourists' and advised that small or large parties could be conveyed to Dovedale. This tourist trade, combined with local social functions, remained the 'bread and butter' of the Green Man throughout the 20th century, but it struggled to survive. Following a period of financial difficulty, it closed its doors in 2012. It remained boarded up until a local businessman saw its potential and bought the property. It was extensively remodelled and renovated and reopened in 2018.

The Greyhound at Cromford (originally the Black Greyhound) was built by Richard Arkwright towards the end of the 18th century as a resting place on the Ashbourne to Chesterfield turnpike and as stabling for the Manchester coach. It also

The Greyhound, Cromford.

served as a lodging for the many visitors to the cotton mills. Arkwright used the inn to reward his workers and promote his business. When John Byng visited in June 1790, he recorded it as, 'cheap and pleasant, with good stabling'. He also noted that the landlord of the Greyhound Inn had under his care 'a grand assortment of prizes from Sir Richard Arkwright to be given at the years end to such bakers and butchers as shall have best furnished the market ... They consist of beds, presses, clocks, chairs and bespeak of Sir Rd's prudence and cunning, for without ready provisions, his colony could not prosper.' Arkwright also used the Greyhound to host the two balls which he gave each year to his workmen and their wives. This was much appreciated by his employees and helped him to recruit and retain an industrious and sober workforce. As a world heritage site, Cromford is today popular with visitors from all over the world, and many of these stay or refresh themselves at the Greyhound.

The Half Moon at Littleover dates back to the latter half of the 16th century. It began life as a farm and alehouse but by the 18th century it served as a coaching inn, the stables of which still survive. Littleover was still very much a village at this time, with a population of around 500. It is not surprising that country sports were popular. Hunting was an important feature of village life and in the 1840s Mr Brearley's Beagles met monthly at the Half Moon. Despite its rural location, the pub featured regularly in the 19th-century records of the magistrate's courts. In January 1884 George Potter,

The Half Moon, Littleover.

alias Hannibal, was charged with refusing to quit the Half Moon when requested to do by the landlady, and with assaulting a police constable in the execution of his duty. Although pleading guilty, he was given a very bad character reference by the Deputy Chief Constable and was committed to prison for 14 days. The harshness of criminal justice at this time is well exemplified by an incident that took place in 1904. In July of that year William Chown, a labourer of no fixed abode, was charged with stealing a knife, value 3d from the Half Moon. It seems that shortly after half past eight in the morning he had called at the pub and asked for a pint of beer and two pennies-worth of bread and cheese. This was served and the knife was lent to him, but after he had left it went missing and the police were informed. He pleaded guilty to the charge and was sent to prison for 14 days with hard labour. In the early years of the 20th century, the Half Moon played an important role in the life of the village. Auction sales, inquests, football matches and flower shows were all held here. In November 1914 a smoking concert was held in aid of the Belgian Relief Fund. During World War Two, the pub's customers collected £1 8s 8d for the Derby and District Fighter Plane Fund, and after the war had ended the Littleover branch of the Royal British Legion held their meetings here. The pub continued to support local and national causes and £5 10s 9d was collected for the Cresswell Colliery Disaster Fund in November 1950. The Half Moon remains an important focal point in the village, where residents gather and socialise.

The Hawk and Buckle in Etwall dates back to the early years of the 19th century. The pub sign is that of a buckled hawk and three twisted hanks of cotton, which indicates that it was originally owned by the Cotton family. It remained so until 1890 when it was sold to Thomson's (later Marston's) Burton Brewery. It lay on the main route between Derby and Uttoxeter and for many years provided stabling and accommodation for weary travellers. A contemporary account records that on one occasion an elephant was stabled here by a visiting circus, which is said to have performed on the village cricket field. The pub benefitted from the arrival of the railway. In September 1880 members of the Burton on Trent Natural History and Archaeological Society organised an excursion to the village. Following a tour of the 16th century almshouses, the local newspaper reported that they 'partook of an excellent tea at the Hawk and Buckle'. In June 1902 the country celebrated the coronation of King Edward VII. Although unsuccessful in obtaining an extension to his licence for the pub, *The Derby Daily Telegraph* of 20 June 1902 reported that the landlord of the Hawk and Buckle had been granted an occasional licence to sell intoxicants in a tent in a field at Etwall where the coronation festivities were being held. During the first half of the 20th century, the Hawk and Buckle hosted a variety of activities including sales and auctions, presentations, wedding receptions and meetings of the local Conservative Association.

The Hawk and Buckle, Etwall.

The Hawk and Buckle remains a popular local pub. It is a free house which serves real ale and home-cooked food.

Hodgkinson's Hotel in Matlock Bath is an historic grade II listed building which dates from 1770. It was previously known as the New Inn and was originally part of the Great Hotel that was built to serve the many visitors who were attracted to the town during the Georgian era to take the waters at Smedley's Hydro. It was subsequently bought by wine merchant Job Hodgkinson in 1830. He developed both a successful wine trade and a brewery on the premises, which used the disused lead mines behind the hotel for the storage of wine. A guide book published in 1851 declared that 'the accommodations at this house are good'. It praised the wine cellars as one of the best in the kingdom and commented on the views of the rocks, green and river which could be seen from the sitting room window. It continues to flourish as a boutique hotel and has been favourably reviewed in the national press.

The Hurt Arms at Ambergate was built in 1874 by Francis Hurt to replace the Thatched House Tavern and Posting House, which was demolished by the Midland Railway to make way for expansion. The club room at the Hurt Arms was used for religious services prior to the building of the church in 1891 and was also the original venue of the annual flower show. During the 19th century the Hurt Arms was frequently used for sales of land, property and livestock. Inquests were also held here and in May

Hodgkinson's Hotel, Matlock Bath.

1903 a strange and rather gruesome enquiry was held here. The skeleton of a man with some shreds of clothing had been found in the river. The police raised the theory that it was the remains of a black man who was alleged to have committed a robbery at a circus when staying in Matlock in November 1891. According to *The Derbyshire Times and Chesterfield Herald,* 'the skeleton lay in a barrow when viewed by the jury and presented a gruesome and sickening spectacle'. Despite extensive enquiries, the coroner declared that this was one of those cases where it was impossible to fathom at an inquest. Following his advice, the jury returned a verdict that 'someone unknown, a male person, had been found dead in the water of the River Derwent at Ambergate but

The Hurt Arms, Ambergate.

how or by what means he came there the evidence did not show'. Business meetings were also held here, although less frequently. In January 1876 the shareholders of the Ambergate Patent Railway Wheel and Wagon Company met here to consider the winding up of the business due to financial difficulties. During the 20th century the pub went through a number of changes of ownership. The Hurt Arms has recently been extensively renovated and describes itself as 'a boutique B&B and stunning industrial wedding venue'.

The King's Head, Buxton, was originally built around 1725 as the manse to the first non-conformist chapel in Buxton. In time, the trustees of the chapel leased the manse as an inn to draw in much needed capital. The present building dates from the middle of the 19th century, although it has the same footprint as the original manse. By the 1850s it was operating as a coaching inn. *The Buxton Advertiser* of 23 May 1857 advised that the Royal Peveril Coach left here for Manchester every morning at half past eight and returned from the Commercial Hotel, Manchester, for Buxton at one pm. A few years later the Celebrity provided a service from the King's Head to Bakewell, Matlock and Cromford before returning to Manchester via Buxton. Other coaches that operated from the King's Head included the Express and Perseverance (to Manchester) and the Sun and Enterprise (to Matlock). A notice in *The Buxton Herald* in June 1853 also advertised 'Phaetons, Flys and neat Pony Carriage always in readiness'. It also

The King's Head, Buxton.

provided post horses, carriages, a lock-up coach house and good stabling. An inquest was held here in 1870 into the death of Luke McDonald, a hawker, who died only a few yards away. It appeared from the evidence that the deceased was standing in the Market Place talking to a companion when suddenly he fell down and expired within three minutes. A verdict of congestive apoplexy of the brain was returned. By 1878 the King's Head was advertising itself as, 'only three minutes' walk from the station' and asserted that, 'Gentlemen and Private Families will find the Hotel replete with every comfort'. The King's Head is a listed building and currently advertises itself as 'a grand old traditional pub with old world charm and a wonderful atmosphere'.

The King's Head in Duffield was in existence from at least the 16th century and it was here that the Enclosure Commissioners met during their investigations and deliberations in 1787-88. Tithe payments were also received here. A notice in *The Derby Mercury* announced that the 'Audit for receiving the tithes for the Old Inclosure of Duffield is fixed for 24th January 1803 at Mr Booth's, the King's Head Inn in Duffield'. As one of the principal inns of the village, it was also used for the billeting of soldiers. The last known incidence of this was around 1880 when a small detachment of cavalry spent the night there. Inquests were also held here. In 1901 the coroner summoned a jury to enquire into circumstances surrounding the death of a person found in a ditch on Milford Road in the village. A variety of social events were

The King's Head, Duffield.

held at the inn. Some of these attracted large numbers of patrons. In 1837 a 'Smoking Concert' was held in a covered court adjoining the hotel when it was reported that 350 persons were present. During the 1860s a carrier service was operated from the premises and in 1861 a notice in *The Derby Mercury* announced that the landlord (John Stanesby) could provide 'covered and open carriages with good horses and careful drivers … at moderate charges'. It seems that the King's Head was a well-conducted house, but in 1829 Silas Porter, the landlord, was fined for having two measures in his house which were 'not according to the standards in the exchequer'. A few years later another landlord, William Toplis, was also fined for a similar breach of the law. An offence of a different nature was reported in 1895 when the landlord (Henry Wild) was accused of using 'filthy and disgusting language to those in the place'. In his defence he stated that he was 'upset through one of his servants having turned off the water and it froze'. Despite this, he was fined 10 shillings! The inn continued to play an important role in the life of the village in the early years of the 20th century. Sales were held here and the Duffield Fire Appliance was kept in an outbuilding adjacent to the pub until the fire station on Snake Lane was built. Offiler's Brewery purchased the King's Head in 1922, but it continued to play an important part in the life of the village for almost a century. The King's Head reopened in August 2018 after being closed for over a year.

The Lion Inn at Belper was probably built in the late 16th or early 17th century and was previously known as the Red Lion. Originally a timber-framed thatched building, it changed considerably in size, style and structure during the following years. A bill of sale of 1824 stated that this inn had two large parlours, five bedrooms, extensive cellars, brewhouse, coach house and stabling for 10 horses. During the 18th century, the Telegraph coach called at the Red Lion every day at one o'clock on its journey from Sheffield to Birmingham and passed through on its return journey at four o'clock. The Lord Nelson from Nottingham stopped at the Red Lion at 9am and returned from Manchester at half past one. In later years other coaches that called there, included the Peveril of the Peak, the Royal Bruce and the Defiance. By the late 1830s as many as twelve coaches were calling daily. In 1840 the railway arrived in Belper and all but one of the coaches ceased to operate. The Red Lion was also a meeting place for the landed gentry of the area. According to a contemporary account on 7 January 1833, a dinner was given to the members of the Southern Division of the County of Derby, at the house of Joseph Deauville, host of the Red Lion Inn, Belper. Dinner was placed on the table at four o'clock and the guests included Lord Waterpark, the Hon George Vernon and several members of the Strutt family. The same account recorded that 'the dinner was well cooked and great plenty of it'. The Hon George Vernon provided the venison and Lord Waterpark, the game. The inn was successful in adapting to the times. The coming of the railway had a devastating effect on the coach trade, but from 1825 a horse-drawn omnibus from the Red Lion attended all trains from the railway station. It is interesting to note that somehow the proprietor of the Red Lion had managed to obtain exclusive rights to this service. The pub suffered a decline in the latter years of the 20th century, but in 2014 new owners refurbished the building and reinstated its hotel and restaurant status.

The Malt at Aston on Trent was originally known as the Malt Shovel and can be traced back to 1857. One of the earliest landlords was John Holbrook. In 1891, at the age of 82, he had already been in charge of the pub for over half a century when he was summoned to appear before Derby County Police Court. Represented by his eldest son, he was charged with allowing drunkenness on his premises. Giving evidence, police constable Badger stated that on the day in question he saw Fannie Henson leaning against the bar very drunk. The witness spoke to the defendant who denied giving any drink to Henson. Henson, however, called him a liar. After considering the evidence the magistrates found him guilty and imposed a fine of 10 shillings and costs. For her part, Fanny Henson was fined 2s 6d with costs for being drunk on licensed premises. Another long-serving landlord was John Ludlow, who held the licence for nearly 30 years, retiring in 1927. In addition to being landlord of the Malt Shovel, he played an active role in village affairs. According to his obituary he was an overseer of the poor in the village and for nearly 30 years was a member of the Parish Council. He was also the auditor of the Loyal Holden Friendly Society. It was in 1902, during his tenure, that

The Malt, Aston on Trent.

the Coronation of King Edward VIII took place. An application for an extension of one hour on the nights of 26 and 27 June was made but refused by the magistrates. George Collis took over the licence in 1927. He was also a plasterer by trade but failed to make a success of either business. He was declared bankrupt in June 1931, blaming 'loss of plastering contracts and taking over a non-paying beer house'! In the 1940s and 1950s the Malt Shovel continued to play its part in the life of the village. A Produce Club was organised, which held its first annual horticultural show and sports at the village recreation ground. The locals were, however, conscious of national issues. In October 1950 they collected £7 for the victims of the Cresswell Colliery Disaster. A few years ago the pub was renamed the Malt and underwent something of a makeover. It is today a popular and successful gastro-pub. It retains a function room and still joins in with the village well dressing when it hosts live music.

The Malt Shovel Inn at Spondon stands on the site of the ancient malt house, which was the source of the 'Great Fire of Spondon' that destroyed most of the village in 1340. It claims, with some justification, to be the oldest site of any licensed premises within the city. The present inn was built in the late-18th or early-19th century, although some parts date from 1680. For many years the Malt Shovel was owned by the Drury-Lowes of Locko Hall, who owned several farms in the area. Tenant farmers would gather at the inn once a year to pay their rents and enjoy the hospitality provided by

The Malt Shovel Inn at Spondon.

the squire. This custom came to an end with the start of rationing in World War Two. The inn was later sold to Offiler's Brewery of Derby. Today the pub retains much of its original character and is listed in the Campaign for Real Ale's National Inventory of Historic Pub Interiors. The room that attracts most attention is a 'snug' that contains a 1920s-style hearth and some rare and unusual high-backed seats which are found in only one other pub in Derbyshire.

The Market Hotel in New Square, Chesterfield, was previously called the Post Office Vaults (1869-72), Market Inn from around 1883, Market Tavern and finally the Market Hotel from about 1892. It has had a largely uneventful history, but at the Derbyshire Winter assize held in February 1885 the landlord, Alfred Redfern, was found guilty of forging a receipt for £15 19s 6d. It seems that in April 1883 he had obtained beer to this value from a Sheffield brewery and had forged a receipt indicating that the bill had been paid. Around the same time that this case came to court, a serious fire broke out at what was then the Market Tavern. *The Derby Daily Telegraph* reported that 'the outbreak was discovered soon after midnight and the Corporation Fire Brigade was soon on the spot. The fire had broken out in the singing room and before it was got under control a valuable piano was destroyed.' The same report noted that the damage was estimated at between £100 and £200 but was entirely covered by insurance. The exterior of the pub remains largely unchanged, but it has adapted to the

The Market Hotel, Chesterfield.

The Mason's Arms, Mickleover.

demands of its 21ˢᵗ-century clientele. It now provides real ale, artisan gin tasting, live entertainment and a menu that includes vegan items.

The Mason's Arms in Mickleover was built in 1724 and is probably the oldest pub in the village. By the early years of the 19ᵗʰ century it was home to a number of local clubs and societies. Sales of a land, property, timber and other items were held here and the Mickleover Friendly Society used the Mason's Arms both for its regular meetings and anniversary celebrations. In June 1881 *The Derby Daily Telegraph*, reporting the anniversary of the society, recorded that after concluding the main business the members formed into a procession headed by the Mickleover Brass Band and paraded the village on their way to a service in the church. It was not unusual for landlords to be found guilty of minor infringements of the licensing laws, but in December 1870, John Brassington, the landlord of the Mason's Arms, was charged with assaulting Henry Dean and stealing from his person a book, a banker's receipt for £600, a purse, a sovereign, two half sovereigns and seven shillings. The evidence against him was compelling and the jury returned a verdict of guilty after deliberating for only a few minutes. The sentence of 10 years' penal servitude created some sensation in court but the judge commented that the charge involved not only a breach of hospitality and care of his guests but was attempted to be covered up by hypocrisy and lying. The case should, he declared, be an example to all publicans! Inquests were also held here in the 19ᵗʰ century. These were usually fairly straightforward, but in December 1889 *The Derby Mercury* reported a 'Mysterious Death at Mickleover'. An inquest was held at the Masons Arms regarding the death of an unknown man who was found dead in a barn in Mickleover. The barn had been nailed up for over three months and the jury returned a verdict of 'found dead without any marks of violence'. A number of local clubs continued to meet here in the 20ᵗʰ century, including an angling club, cricket club and the Manor Lodge of the Royal Ancient Order of Buffaloes. Many of the locals served in the armed forces during World War Two, but those left behind did their bit to support the war effort. In November 1940 the pub contributed £2 19s 8d to the Derby and District Fighter Plane Fund. The Mason's Arms is owned by Punch Taverns and was recently refurbished.

The Midland Hotel in Derby was only the second purpose-built railway hotel in the country and is thought to be unique in having been in continuous use since its opening in 1841. The building was designed by Francis Thompson. It has been described as having the character and refinement of an elegant country house with classical Italianate proportions; and in 1842 *Glover's Directory* referred to 'upwards of fifty superior bedrooms, and numerous dining and sitting-rooms'. It generally attracted a better class of traveller including the gentry and the nobility and this was reflected in its charges. In 1843 a bed for the night cost four shillings, and if you were accompanied

The Midland Hotel, Derby.

by a servant a bed for him or her was charged at two shillings. In the morning a breakfast with chops and eggs could be had for three shillings. Queen Victoria and her family stayed here overnight in 1849 on her way north to Balmoral. From 1875 the hotel also provided luncheon baskets for the benefit of railway passengers. Priced at three shillings, these contained 'Half a chicken, with Ham or Tongue, Salad, Bread, Cheese, Butter ... and a Half-Bottle of Claret or Burgundy'. For the less affluent, a smaller basket was available at two shillings. This contained veal and ham pie with salad, bread, cheese, butter and a bottle of stout. This service was very popular and was soon copied by other railway hotels throughout the country. In 1887 the Midland even introduced a 'hot basket meal', which contained a chop, vegetables and wine or stout! During the 20th century the Midland Hotel remained a prestigious venue and a wide range of social and business functions were held there. Today it is part of the Hallmark group of hotels.

The Midland Hotel, Matlock Bath, dates from the Victorian era and was probably built sometime after the arrival of the North Midland Railway in 1849. Business increased with the growing tourist popularity of the town. At the Brewster Sessions held in August 1869, Miss Eleanor Smedley, the proprietress, applied for a spirit licence. Her solicitor contended that the large influx of visitors and excursionists to Matlock Bath had rendered an increase in middle-class hotel accommodation necessary and

The Midland, Matlock Bath.

called the stationmaster of Matlock Bath and others to prove this. The Bench granted the licence. A number of staff were employed at the hotel including cook, general servant, bar staff and housekeeper It was not unusual for one individual to fulfil a number of duties. In May 1899 a notice in *The Derbyshire Times and Chesterfield Herald* advertised for 'a respectable young person as Housemaid-Waitress to assist in bar'. Good references were required and it was stated that an appointment would be made on the basis of a personal interview. As one of the principal establishments in the town, the Midland Hotel was the venue for sales of land and property, although in June 1879 an unusual lot, the Devonshire Cavern, was offered for sale by auction. In the 1930s the Matlock and District Football League held their meetings there and in 1935 the landlord, Frank George, revived the Whitworth Cup Quoits Competition to raise funds for the Whitworth Hospital in Darley Dale. Social functions were also held here during this period. In November 1933 the staff of the Masson Mills held their annual dinner there. For most of the remainder of the century the Midland had an uneventful history, although there were one or two incidents of violent behaviour which were reported in the local press. The Midland is an Enterprise Inns free house with an attractive location backing on to the river.

The Miners Arms at Brassington has close links with the early lead mining industry. Brassington was an important centre of lead mining in the 18th and 19th centuries. For a number of years, the miners' special Barmote Court met here and more than one landlord was also barmaster of the Brassington Liberty. He sat with a jury of 24 fellow miners to record claims, measure the ore, settle disputes and collect the royalties and tithes that were payable to the Crown and to the Church. Like other pubs in the area, the Miners Arms played an important role in extending credit to miners and others. Many of the local lead miners were poor and scratched only a basic living from a combination of farming and lead mining. They often needed support to start a new mine or purchase equipment. Pub records for the Miners Arms show that at various times the landlord provided credit for food and drink. Miners generally drank ale, although there are also entries in the accounts for gin, brandy and rum as well as 'rum and watter'. The opening of a new mine was often the cause of celebration and one entry in the account book records five shillings and sixpence for 'ale & fiddling'. From at least the 18th century, a Men's Friendly Society held their meetings at the Miners Arms. In 1808 John Farey reported that '120 members assembled in the fore-noon to transact their business in their meeting room'. They then processed through the town before returning to the Miners Arms for dinner. Later in the century an Odd Fellows Lodge (a successor to the Men's Friendly Society) also met at the pub where the landlord kept the membership and account books. Over the years the Miners Arms was also used for sales and auctions, manorial courts, inquests and a variety of social functions. Today it is one of only two pubs in the village. It remains popular with both tourists and local residents. Little changed outside; the interior comprises just one room divided by a fireplace.

The Old Hall Hotel in Buxton was built by the Sixth Earl of Shrewsbury in 1572-1573 and was described at the time as 'a very goodly house, four square, four storeys high, with a great chamber and other goodly lodgings to about thirty'. The main purpose of the Old Hall was to provide a safe house for the visits of Mary, Queen of Scots, who came here to take the waters. She stayed here at least five times between 1573 and 1584,

although Queen Elizabeth remained suspicious of her cousin and forbade all visitors not approved by Shrewsbury. On her last visit she scratched a Latin inscription on one of the windows. In translation this read: 'Buxton, whose warm waters have made thy name famous, perchance I shall visit thee no more'. Perhaps she had a premonition of her own death as only three years later she was executed. The Old Hall was also patronised by other members of the Elizabethan court including Lord Burghley, Sir Thomas Smith, Lord Gilbert, Lady

Plaque outside the Old Hall Hotel.

The Old Hall Hotel, Buxton.

Mary Talbot and the Earl of Leicester. It seems that the building was initially not well maintained, as in 1681 Charles Cotton recorded that the hall was 'near a ruin' until rebuilt by the 3rd Duke of Devonshire around 1670. This 'rebuilding' retained much of the original structure behind the extension and new façade. Although the building was regarded as handsome, early writers were critical of both the accommodation and the food. Edward Brown, who came here in 1681, considered the 'mutton like dog'. Celia Fiennes, who came just a few years later in 1697, complained that 'the beer they allow you at the meals is so bad that little can be drank'. She was also critical of the sleeping arrangements and declared that 'sometimes they are so crowded that three lye in a bed'. Daniel Defoe stayed in Buxton in 1778 during his tour of Great Britain. Of the Old Hall he wrote: 'The Duke of Devonshire has built a large handsome house at the bath, where there is convenient lodging, and very good provisions.' Only a few years later, the 5th Duke built the impressive Crescent complex of buildings and Buxton became an established Spa town that attracted people from all over the country. In 1791 the hotel was leased to James Cumming. He was well-connected socially and guests included bishops and members of the aristocracy. The Old Hall has remained a hotel ever since and has attracted famous guests from all over the world.

The Old Sun Inn on the High Street in Buxton was built in the 17th century to serve as a coaching inn. It claims to be the second-oldest building in the town. The exterior is

The Old Sun Inn, Buxton.

little changed and an arched passageway leading to a yard at the rear is still inscribed with the words 'Good Stabling'. For many years a warehouse stood close by. This was used by carriers and undoubtedly brought additional business to the inn. Trade directories of the period suggest that the Old Sun Inn was not a major staging post for coaches, although in the 1850s the *Wonder* operated a daily service from the Sun Inn to the Angel in Manchester. It did, however, take advantage of the opportunities to serve the local tourist trade. A notice in *The Buxton Advertiser* on 9 October 1869 advertised 'Cheap Excursions to Castleton and Back'. The Peveril of the Peak left the Sun Inn at 9.45am for Castleton 'allowing time to see the Ebbing and Flowing Well, Peak Cavern, Speedwell Mine, Blue John Mine, Peveril Castle &c, &c and all the beautiful scenery of the neighbourhood'. Return fare was 3s 6d outside and 4s 6d inside. A few years later an omnibus service left the Sun every day for Taddington, Ashford, Bakewell, Haddon Hall, Rowsley and Chatsworth. At around this time the landlord, Richard Stubbs, attempted to attract custom by advertising 'well aired beds, good stabling and lock up coach houses' as well as 'a choice and well-selected stock of beverages'. The Old Sun Inn remains a popular local pub. The *Lonely Planet Guide* describes it as 'the cosiest of Buxton's pubs' with 'a warren of rooms full of original features'.

The Palace Hotel in Buxton was designed by Henry Currey and built in 1864-6 as a speculative investment by a joint stock company at a cost of nearly £50,000. Curry

The Palace Hotel, Buxton.

himself was one of the investors and he designed the 105-room hotel in the French chateau style, with a central tower, on an elevated site adjacent to the railway station. The company failed after only a year but was bought back by a consortium composed largely of the original investors. In the years that followed it established itself as one of the most popular and successful hotels in Buxton. During World War One it became an annexe of the Granville Military Hospital (itself previously the Buxton Hydro). At the conclusion of hostilities, it returned to its previous status and during the 1920s and 1930s, along with other hotels in the town, it became a centre of the high- class conference trade. This conference trade continued after World War Two. The National Union of Teachers was just one of a number of organisations which held their annual conferences in the town and senior delegates were frequently accommodated at the Palace Hotel. It continued to adapt to the times and in the 1950s well-known football clubs such as Manchester United,

The Patten Makers Arms, Duffield.

Manchester City and Nottingham Forest stayed here when they came to Buxton to take advantage of the 'water treatment' to tone up players for matches. Today the Palace Hotel is the largest hotel in Buxton and attracts a large number of British and international guests.

The Patten Makers Arms in Duffield was originally a stone building but was replaced by the present two-storey brick building in the middle of the 19th century. Its name stems from the patten makers who worked in the adjoining forges. Pattens were metal devices that elevated shoes above the dirt and mud of the streets at this time. In 1840 the pub was owned by the Reverend

Pub sign, the Patten Makers Arms.

William Barber but the landlord was Samuel Lovatt, who was listed as a blacksmith and beer retailer in a directory of 1849. Other landlords were similarly listed as having a second occupation. In 1861 Thomas Renwick was listed as patten-ring maker and beer-house keeper. When he died, however, in 1881 he was described in his will only as a patten maker and not a beer-house keeper. The pub was advertised for lease in 1897 when it was described as containing a 'bar, tap-room, smoke room, living room, 3 bedrooms, store closet, pantry, scullery, room over, and cellar, coal house, chamber over, shed (for 5 cows and 1 horse and chop place) loft over, pig stye, manure pit, garden at rear'. During the early years of the 20th century the pub was used for sales and auctions as well as inquests and meetings of the local Oddfellows lodge. By the 1920s and 1930s it hosted a wide range of organisations and activities including an annual flower and vegetable show, meetings of the local Conservative Association and wedding receptions. In 2014 the business was crowned the Country Pub of the Year and has been in *The Good Beer Guide* for a number of years.

The Peacock Hotel at Rowsley was originally known as Rowsley Manor and was built in 1652 as the private residence for John Stevenson, agent to the Manners family. The carved stone peacock above the porch is part of the family crest. After briefly becoming the dower house to nearby Haddon Hall, it was converted into a hotel in the 1820s. Its opening coincided with the closing of two other inns (the Nag's Head and the Red Lion) in the village. From the outset the Peacock attracted the

The Peacock Hotel, Rowsley.

local aristocracy and representatives of the highest echelons of society. In June 1899 the Marquis of Granby stayed there whilst angling on the nearby River Wye. Other visitors included the Dukes of Rutland and Devonshire, who enjoyed a variety of country sports in the area. They were often joined by the younger sons of other families. In August 1923 these included Lord Gerald Wellesley (second son of the Duke of Wellington) and Lord Ivor Chamberlain (second son of the Duke of Marlborough). It seems that not all visitors were equally welcome. In March 1903 the licensing magistrates at Bakewell heard complaints that

The Peacock at Chesterfield.

bone fide travellers had been refused 'reasonable refreshments' at the Peacock. The hotel has continued to attract celebrity visitors (particularly when filming in the area). In recent years these have included Keira Knightley, Ralph Feinnes and Dame Judy Dench.

The Peacock at Chesterfield is currently a coffee lounge. The building was constructed around 1500 and may have belonged to one of the two wealthy guilds of medieval Chesterfield – the Guild of the Blessed Mary or the Guild of the Holy Cross. By the 1690s it had passed out of public ownership and had become the house and shop of a family of wealthy merchants. They sold a variety of goods ranging from high value spices such as nutmeg, cloves and cinnamon to more mundane necessities including candles, pipes, pins and thread. For around two centuries it was occupied by a succession of owners and at some point it was divided into three properties. By 1829 it had become a public house 'called or known by the sign of the Peacock'. By the 1850s the pub was well established in the town. Sales and auctions were held here as well as meetings of friendly societies. A major fire in February 1974 revealed the original timber framing. In 1981 it was restored for use as the Peacock Information and Heritage Centre. After this was relocated to a specially built Tourist Information Centre, the building became the Peacock Coffee Lounge.

The Portland Hotel in West Bars, Chesterfield, can trace its origins back to the building of the Lancashire, Derbyshire and East Coast Railway with its new station on

The Portland Hotel, Chesterfield.

West Bars, which was opened in March 1897. A number of buildings were demolished to make way for the railway and these included two inns, the White Horse and the Bird-in-Hand. In April of the following year William Stones Brewery submitted plans for a new hotel to be erected on the site of the two inns, to be known as the Hotel Portland. Its name derived from the Duke of Portland on whose estates much of the railway was built. The new hotel was opened in December 1899 by Lord Roseberry (Prime Minister 1894-95). Its licence was transferred from the White Horse, as was the first landlord. It was an impressive building built to attract the great and the good of Chesterfield as well as a wide range of travellers arriving at the new railway station. A guide to the town, published shortly before the official opening, declared that 'the building will be fitted with electric light, and the sanitary arrangements will be carried out on the most modern principles, no effort being spared to render the hotel a first-class family and commercial centre'. Public rooms included a restaurant, a large dining room suitable for private parties and smoke, billiard, coffee and commercial rooms. In an attempt to attract a wider clientele a separate entrance on the Park Road end of the building led to a refreshment room and a second-class smoking room. It was made clear that this part of the building was 'entirely distinct from the remainder of the hotel'. From the outset the hotel succeeded in attracting the political and social elite of the town. The Corporation entertained the Mayor here in 1901, 1903 and 1904, and the Scarsdale Freemason's Lodge held their Anniversary Dinner here in 1901. Other local organisations made their home here in the early years of the 20th century, including the Bowling Club and Chesterfield Motor Cycle Club. The hotel was sold to the Brampton Brewery in April 1925 for £16,750. It later became a free house and is now part of the Wetherspoons chain.

The Punch Bowl Inn at West Hallam was built as a farm house in the mid-18th century and became a pub some time later. For many years it was at the heart of local activities. A typical village pub, it provided a home for numerous local organisations and societies including the Rural Society, the Garden Society and the local football club. Indeed, for many years the players used the pub as their changing rooms. The East Derbyshire Farmers' Club held their annual show here and ploughing competitions were held in a field adjoining the pub. By the latter years of the 19th century a cabbage club had been formed, which held its annual dinner at the pub. On 8 December 1859 Francis Alexander Newdigate, son of the village squire, was married. Local celebrations included a fine dinner at the Punch Bowl, which was attended by 42 farmers and principle tradesmen from the village. During World War Two, soldiers were billeted in the upper room of the inn. The landlord also contributed to the war effort by raising pigs to supplement rationing. The pub benefitted from an increase in trade following the building of a large

The Punch Bowl, West Hallam.

The Railway Inn, Belper.

housing estate in the 1970s. In 1989 a restaurant was added which served a very popular Sunday lunch accompanied by a traditional sweet trolley. It remains an important village asset and is still used for a variety of social functions.

The Queens Head at Little Eaton dates back to 1835. It was for many years a coaching inn. It was originally known as the Delvers Inn after the 'delvers' who worked in the local quarry. Early in the 20th century it was renamed the Kings Head but became the Queen's Head following the coronation of Queen Elizabeth II in 1953.

The Railway in King Street, Belper, was built in the 1880s, replacing an earlier pub called the Tiger. It probably took its name from the North Midland Railway which opened a station nearby in 1840. A notice that appeared in *The Derby Daily Telegraph* in June 1882 described it as adjoining the Midland Railway Station and being fitted and furnished in the most complete style and every accommodation for visitors. It boasted 'one of Burroughs and Watts best billiard tables' and stabling for 15 horses.

In 1891 a notice advised that the hotel offered 'excellent accommodation for cyclists, pedestrians and travellers'. The hotel was very proud of its billiard table and some years later the appearance of a horse in the billiard room caused some consternation. *The Belper News* from 2 October 1896 reported that having taken fright the horse rushed straight into the doorway of the hotel, bursting open the doors. It dashed up the passage and into the billiard room. The same newspaper reported that 'no damage was done beyond the breaking of a little crockery which was dragged off a table and the animal escaped with a slight cut'. It seems that 'great alarm was caused in the house but fortunately no one was in the way of the frightened steed'! During the early years of the 20th century it fulfilled many of the functions of a typical small-town hotel. It was a popular venue for the local inhabitants of the town to enjoy a drink, and sales and auctions were also held here. On occasions the inn yard was used for the sale of livestock. On 14 March 1884 a notice in *The Derbyshire Advertiser and Journal* announced a sale by auction of '5 horses, 6 sets of harness, Gig, Dog Cart, Brake, Cabs, Carriages, Heavy Cart and 11 fat pigs' On 22 March 1884 the Railway Inn also provided accommodation for the coroner's courts. In May 1903 *The Derby Daily Telegraph* reported 'A Servant Girl's Sad End'. An inquest held at the Railway Inn enquired into the death of Mary Ethel Glew, a 16-year-old servant at the Kings Head, whose body had been found floating in the river. Witnesses stated that she had appeared upset and had been seen 'crying bitterly'. There was, however, no evidence to show how she came to be in the water and a verdict of 'found drowned' was recorded. The Belper Anglers' Club also met here and in December 1902 the landlord applied for an extension of one hour to accommodate their annual dinner. By the 1930s and 1940s the Railway was still playing an important role in the life of the community. In December 1930 a smoking concert was held there under the auspices of Belper Men's Conservative Association, when they were addressed by Mr Herbert Wragg, the prospective parliamentary candidate for the Belper Division. During the same period a number of sporting and social clubs held their meetings and sometimes their annual dinners here. At the time of writing there were plans to rename the pub the Pig and Platform. The owners intend to take it 'upmarket' and create a modern premium bar 'to meet different customer needs throughout the day'.

The Red Lion at Wirksworth probably dates from the Middle Ages but was rebuilt in 1770 as a coaching and posting inn on the Ashbourne turnpike. It offered generous stabling at the rear as well as its own bowling green. It once housed the assembly rooms for the town's civic and social functions prior to the town hall being built. Regular assemblies were held here and in 1815 a celebration was held at the Red Lion to mark the defeat of Napoleon. A number of important local organisations held their meetings at the inn, including the Wirksworth Farmers' Club, the Wirksworth

The Red Lion, Wirksworth.

Association for Prosecuting Felons, the local Floral & Horticultural Society and the Trustees of the Wirksworth and Hulland Ward and Idridgehay and Duffield Turnpike Roads. The Inclosure Commissioners met here in May 1836 for the purpose of 'proceeding in the business of the inclosure generally and particularly to hear any objections or suggestions to make relative to any work, matters or any things being done or to be done'. The ghost of a coachman is said to haunt the Red Lion. He was attempting to guide his coach through the archway when the horses suddenly panicked and dashed forward. Unable to move his head in time, he was decapitated. Ever since, the spectre of a headless man has haunted the pub. The Red Lion has kept up with the times and now houses a micro-pub, the Firkin in the Lion, within its premises.

The Royal Oak in the ancient Shambles area of Chesterfield claims to be the oldest pub in the town and possibly one of the oldest in in the country. A sign on the outside of the pub states: 'The Royal Oak was built in the 12th century. This was one of the oldest inns in Chesterfield & one of the oldest in England. It was formerly a rest house for the Knights Templar on the years of the Holy Crusades. Then through, and after the Medieval period it was used as two butcher's shops & inn accommodation. The earliest discovered records show it already being an inn in 1722 A.D.' The Royal Oak was entirely rebuilt in 1748 and then extensively restored in 1898 after the Bateson family sold it to William Stones Brewery. It closed briefly in 2015 but has since reopened.

The Royal Oak, Chesterfield.

The Royal Oak in Ockbrook is the oldest public house in the village and dates back to 1760. It was at first a private house but a few years later it was bought by William Peat, a local weaver who turned it into a public house. From the outset it played an important role in the life of the local community. The Ockbrook Male Friendly Society, established in 1814, held their meetings there. Each year the society held a feast on Whit Sunday and this too was held at the Royal Oak. In the 1840s the Dale Abbey Society for the Prosecution of Felons began to meet here for their annual dinners. Rent

The Rutland Arms, Bakewell.

dinners were also held here when local landowners sat down to dine with their tenants before collecting the year's rent. In the 19th century it was common for landlords to supplement their income with additional employment. John Peat, who was the landlord in the 1850s, was a farmer and butcher as well as a publican. The Royal Oak remained in the hands of the Peat family until 1898 when, following the death of Henry Peat, it was sold by his widow to Offiler's Brewery for £3,920. During World War One six German prisoners were billeted here in the Assembly Room. Brewery mergers led to changes in ownership. Offiler's sold out to Charringtons in 1965. Charringtons merged with Bass in 1967.The same family have run the pub since 1953 and owned it outright since 1989.

The Rutland Arms at Bakewell replaced the White Horse Inn. This was visited by John Byng in 1789 when he described the inn as 'a very good one' where 'the landlady instantly brought before me a quarter of cold ham, a cold duck, salad, tarts and jellies'. He returned a year later and was less complimentary. On this occasion he had cold ham and cold veal pie for supper but complained that he was 'never in a nastier house, or a more gloomy place; everything dirty, and offensive to the smell'! Nor did he have a very good night's sleep, for he wrote: 'I often arose from my very bad bed to look at the weather; which was very rainy, and continued so until near morning'. The present Rutland Arms was constructed in 1804 by the Duke of Rutland. It was built at a time

Crest above the Rutland Arms.

when the Duke was attempting to develop Bakewell as a spa town to rival Buxton. It is claimed that Jane Austin stayed here in 1811 when she was writing *Pride and Prejudice* and that Bakewell provided the inspiration and model for the market town of Lambton in her novel. Other visitors have included the painter Turner, Lord Byron, Charles Dickens, Samuel Coleridge and William Wordsworth. The Rutland Arms was for many years an important social centre in the town. On 28 May 1831 a public dinner was held here to celebrate the King's birthday. The cost was five shillings each. The proceedings started at 5pm and music was provided by Tideswell Band. It was an impressive occasion with a toast list that was 13 items long! A Farmers' Club, which was founded in 1843, held its meetings here once a month to discuss farming methods and new procedures. They later established the famous Bakewell Show. *The Gem of the Peak*, a guide book published in 1851, was lavish in its praise. It described the inn as 'one of the most extensive and best conducted inn in the Kingdom' and noted that it had recently undergone a complete repair. The rooms had been refurnished in 'an elegant and tasty manner' and 'additional conveniences added, so as to promote the comfort and pleasure of the visitors'. Added to this, all parties visiting the inn had 'free liberty to enjoy the sport of angling in the beautiful Wye'. For some years Roman Catholic services were held over the stables of the inn until 1890 when they were able to build their own place of worship in the town. The Rutland Arms still welcomes visitors to the Peak District. Some of the rooms are named after the hotel's famous visitors, including Dickens, Jane Austen, Byron and Turner.

The Seven Stars, Derby.

The Seven Stars in King Street is one of the oldest pubs in Derby. The building dates from 1680 and stands on a site previously occupied by St Helen's Priory. The precise date that it started to operate as a pub is uncertain, as is the date when it became known as the Seven Stars. It was previously known as the Plough, although the sign may have been the celestial phenomenon rather than the agricultural implement. Some believe that the stars originated as the stars of a halo round the head of the Virgin Mary, the mother of Christ. Although not a coaching inn, it did have its own stables and employed an ostler. During World War One it was difficult to find men to do this work and an advert for an ostler placed in 1916 specified that the man had to be ineligible for military service. Until the 1920s it was popular with farmers, particularly on market days when they left their horses to be cared for in the inn yard while they conducted their business in the town. Some idea of the size and status of the Seven Stars can be gleaned from a notice in *The Derby Daily Telegraph* in August 1887 when it advertised 'good beds, large club or dancing room and first-class stabling'. During the 19th century a bowls club met here and an annual Gooseberry Show took place at the inn until at least 1825. The area around the Seven Stars was for many years prone to flooding and *The Derby Mercury* of 27 October 1875 reported that a man who was rather the worse for wear 'provoked jeers and rough jokes of the crowd by his ridiculous endeavours to rescue some of the barrels which were floating in an outhouse'. The Seven Stars was the last pub in Derby to brew its own beer before the recent advent of micro-pubs.

The Shakespeare Inn.

The Shakespeare Inn at Shardlow is a Grade II-listed building and dates from the early years of the 19th century. It is located on the main road through the village and originally had its own stables at the rear of the property. The pub had its own bowling green which was used as the home ground by the Shardlow Bowling Club, who also held their annual dinners at the Shakespeare. During the 19th century the pub was also used for the sale of land and property and inquests were held here from time to time. The half-yearly rent audits of the Shardlow Hall Estate were held here, at which the tenants were treated to a substantial dinner paid for by the landowner and provided by the landlord and landlady of the pub.

The Old Spa Inn on Abbey Street, Derby, was built in 1733 by Dr William Chancey. Constructed around a mineral spa, he hoped to be able to compete with Buxton and Matlock. In order to achieve his ambition, he built a handsome cold bath, changing rooms, a rest room and pleasure walk. Sadly, Chancey died just three years later and his dream never came to fruition. The building became a private residence but in 1832 was converted to an inn. The inn was refurbished and opened out in the 1980s and further improvements were carried out at the start of this century. Traces of Chancey's bath still survive and a survey of 2011 found what appeared to be a sunken bath, suggesting that the system may have been based on a Roman bath house.

The Spread Eagle at Etwall began life as a simple ale house. It was in existence by 1746 when it was owned by a cordwainer and shoemaker by the name of William

Clark. During the 18th and 19th centuries a wide range of business was conducted here. In 1796 meetings were held here to consider the enclosure of common and waste ground. Sales and auctions were held and advertisements appeared in the local press offering the service of stallions to cover mares. Meetings of the Sir John Port's Charities were regularly held at the Spread Eagle. In August 1867 a public dinner was held there to celebrate the passing of an Act for the future management of the Sir John Port's Charity Estates. *The Derby Mercury* reported that between 50 and 60 gentlemen were present, for whom the most generous provision was made by Mr Hardy, the landlord. The pub was also the centre of public rejoicing in the village. Following the defeat of Napoleon in 1814 local celebrations concluded with a ball at the Spread Eagle. According to *The Derby Mercury* it was respectably attended and the dancing was kept up until a late hour. It must have been a great party as the same newspaper reported that 'the liquor not being all drank, dancing again commenced on Friday and continued until dark'! The premises were not always well conducted and the local newspapers contain a number of reports of petty crime and the infringement of licensing laws. By the latter years of the 19th century the Spread Eagle was used for social and political meetings of the local Conservative Association. In November 1898 *The Derby Mercury* reported that a 'largely attended and highly successful smoking concert' was held under the auspices of the local Conservative Association. Music and other entertainment was interspersed with political speeches. The meeting ended with cheers for Mr Gretton, the local Member of Parliament, and the singing of the National Anthem. The Spread Eagle also hosted meetings of the local branch of the Independent Order of Oddfellows. Meetings were held here on a Saturday evening for over a century until it was wound up at some time in the 1940s. During the early years of the 20th century the inn continued to play an important role in the business and social life of the village. By the 1930s in addition to a saloon bar and snug the Spread Eagle boasted a billiards room with full-size billiards table; though the landlady (Clara Marsh) restricted admission to those customers who she deemed 'respectable'. Food was not available at this time though bread and cheese might be provided for passing lorry drivers. The pub also organised a savings club for mixed-company coach outings. These were well supported at a time when few ordinary people could afford to own a motor car. Unfortunately, the outbreak of the World War Two in 1939 resulted in petrol rationing which put an end to such excursions. Later in the war an influx of servicemen, including Americans from the supply depot at nearby Hilton, brought increased custom to the Spread Eagle as well as other pubs in the area. The post-war period also saw a house-building boom in the village. The local population increased from 1,065 in 1951 to 2,740 only 30 years later. This increase in population brought improved business to the Spread Eagle and other pubs in the village. In recent years the Spread Eagle has been described as a modern free house, popular with locals of all ages. It comprises a large single room with a central horseshoe bar.

The Stanhope Arms at Bretby is a listed building with a long history as a pub, restaurant and hotel. It was originally part of the Earl of Carnarvon's estate (to 1921) but has been substantially enlarged since. Some idea of the size and structure of the pub can be gleaned from a sale notice published in 1921. This advised that:

> 'The INN contains
> Basement – commodious Cellerage, large kitchen and Dairy – Larder with back entrance
> Ground Floor – Front Entrance Hall and Staircase, Bar, bar parlour, Tap Room and large Smoking room (with removeable partition for dividing into two rooms)
> First Floor – Four Bedrooms and Lumber Room (off landing)
> In House Yard – Coal house, WC, EC and Urinal
> The OUT-Buildings comprise Two Pigsties, Swill cistern etc; Two-stall Stable, Three Loose Boxes, Carriage House, Harness Room, Calf House and Implement Shed'

The same advertisement also noted that it was an important stopping place on the Burton and Ashby Light Railway. This was a tramway system that linked the towns of Ashby and Burton on Trent via Swadlincote, and operated from 1906 until 1927. The Stanhope Arms was for many years one of the most prestigious venues in the area. In September 1919 *The Derby Journal and Advertiser* reported that the discharged and demobilised soldiers in Bretby were entertained to dinner there by the kind invitation of Mr Herbert Wragg, a wealthy local industrialist. In the 1960s and 1970s it was regarded as a smart place to be seen and several local professional organisations, including the National Union of Teachers, held their annual dinner dances and other social events there. The Stanhope Arms has seen a number of changes in ownership and style but is today part of the Table Table chain of pubs owned by the Whitbread Brewery. It also provides accommodation under the Premier Inns brand.

The Sun Inn, Chesterfield, dates from 1912 and was constructed on the site of an earlier 'Sun Inn' which was built in the 18th century. The inn was used as a collection point by carriers who transported a variety of goods in and out of Chesterfield. Sales of land, livestock and various other items were frequently held here. In June 1902 a notice in the local newspaper offered for sale a wagonette with a moveable head to carry eight. Interested parties were directed to apply to the ostler at the inn. A year later, *The Derbyshire Times and Chesterfield Herald* reported on the attempted suicide of Joseph White, the ostler at the Sun Inn. He had cut his throat from ear to ear with a razor. It seems that his injuries were only superficial as a doctor was later able to

The Sun Inn, Chesterfield.

stich the wound. It emerged later that he had been involved with others in the theft of materials from his employer. A large number of organisations held their meetings here including the Chesterfield and District Boot Trades Association, the local Farmers and Dairymen's Association and the Derbyshire Miners' Association. The Sun Inn is reputedly the most haunted pub in Chesterfield. One evening in 1957 bottles were smashed and barrels moved around in a locked cellar. These strange happenings were blamed on a ghostly coachman whose murdered body was thrown down a well in the cellar in the 18th century. There have also been reports of ghostly footsteps walking around the building. It was sold by John Smith's to the Mansfield Brewery in the 1980s and is now a Marston's pub. It retains its original facade and is a popular venue for live music.

The Swan Inn at Buxton was built in the early years of the 19th century and was originally known as the Malt Shovel. According to local legend the reason for the name change lies in an unfortunate incident which took place around 1850. It is said that the landlord unjustly accused a young soldier of not paying for his drink. Despite his protestations and the comments of the other customers, the landlord frog marched him from the pub, tied him to a tree and brutally flogged him. The outraged locals, appalled by such a brutal act, decided to boycott the inn. Sometime later a new landlord took over and changed the name of the pub in an attempt to create a fresh start for the business.

The Swan Inn, Buxton.

The Tiger Inn is located in Lock Up Yard, just off the Cornmarket in Derby. It was built in 1737 and initially operated as a coaching inn. Stage coaches with flamboyant names such as the Defiance, the Times, the Champion and the Royal Bruce provided regular services to London, Birmingham, Manchester and Nottingham. The Derby Society of Musicians held their meetings here in the latter years of the 18th century. The Tiger endeavoured to keep up with the times and the changing needs of travellers. *Glover's History and Directory of the Borough of Derby* published in 1843 contained a notice from the Tiger Inn which advertised 'Excellent accommodation for commercial gentlemen, good stabling, lock up Gig Houses – Flies and Gigs at the shortest notice – Railway and coach office – The omnibuses call to and from the Station on the arrival and departure of every train'. As a hostelry of some status, the Tiger hosted dinners of prominent local organisations such as the South Derbyshire Agricultural Association and the local Conservative Association. When a Conservative Ball was held at the Derby Assembly Rooms in 1841 the supper was provided by Mrs Taylor of the Tiger Inn. An extension had been built to the inn around 1795. This included an assembly room with orchestra gallery which was still being used in the 1930s. In the decades that followed the Tiger declined in popularity and was much reduced in size. Today it occupies a much smaller site at the end of Lock-up Yard close to the entrance of the Market Hall. Despite its inner-city location it remains very much a community pub.

The Vernon Arms at Sudbury was built by George Vernon as a coaching inn in 1671. The stables were through an archway at the side of the building. It also played an

The Tiger Inn, Derby.

important role in serving the needs of the estate village and members of the surrounding farming communities. Sales and auctions were held at the inn and for many years the local police court met here. Hare coursing was a popular country pursuit in the area and meetings were regularly held in the village. This involved the use of greyhounds which were tested on their ability to run, overtake and turn a hare rather than a form of hunting aiming to capture game. Dogs were sometimes entered for these contests at

The Vernon Arms, Sudbury.

the Vernon Arms, and following one such meeting *The Derby Mercury* reported that upwards of 60 gentlemen sat down to a dinner at the inn. The building is little changed externally and visitors can still see the marks on the stone wall, worn away by the leather breaches of the ostler's boy, who sat on the stone ledge waiting for the Red Rover coach from Lichfield. The Vernon Arms crest is just above the main entrance. It remains the centre of village social life with various games evenings held through the week, including darts, dominoes and even poker.

The Victoria Inn, on Midland Place, Derby, opened in 1857 and may have been built as a speculative venture, as *The Derby Mercury* of 23 April 1856 contained a notice advertising: 'to be let and entered upon immediately, that very commodious and well-arranged house, the Victoria Inn situate in Midland Place contiguous to the Railway Station in Derby'. Because of its proximity to the railway station, the members of the Midland Railway Cab Stand held their annual dinners there. These were supported and sponsored by many of the most important members of society in the town, including the Mayor, local Members of Parliament and other men of standing. *The Derby Mercury* of 3 March 1897 reported on the fifth annual dinner when 'a capital dinner was served by Mr Blackwell to which ample justice was done'. During the evening 'some capital songs were rendered' and the health of the donors was later drunk with musical honours. The meeting concluded with the singing of the National Anthem and the newspaper

The Victoria Inn, Derby.

reported that 'the balance in hand has been placed to the credit of the cabman's sick fund'. The inn was also patronised by local pigeon fanciers and men employed at the locomotive and carriage and wagon works. From time to time retirement and other presentations were made here. In the early years of the 20th century the Victoria also hosted the King Edward IV Lodge of the Royal Ancient Order of Buffalos. This was a friendly society with some similarity to freemasonry. A notice in *The Derby Telegraph* on 15 June 1917 reported that, 'a large and appreciative audience of brethren attended ... to witness the raising of Bros G Elvidge and F Lyman to the

The Vine, Mickleover.

degree of Primo'. It seems that for most of its history this was a respectable and well-run establishment but a note in the rate book, dated 27 August 1933, states that: 'Under the old management this inn was a resort of prostitutes'. Little is known of the Victoria during World War Two, although in April 1944 the landlady, Elsie May Unwin, was fined £1 at Derby Police Court for displaying lights during black-out hours. The Victoria Inn is now part of the Admiral Taverns pub chain. It still benefits from its location, generating foot fall from commuters, students and rail users. A recently refurbished function room provides accommodation for private events and live music.

The Vine on Uttoxeter Road, Mickleover, opened around the middle of the 19th century, possibly originally as a beer house. It is believed that the first landlord was also a wheelwright. Inquests were held here as well as some of the other licensed premises in the village. Sadly and unusually, however, in February 1888 an inquest was held into the death of the landlord, Matthew Clarke, who had been found hanging from a rope in a neighbouring cowshed. During the latter years of the 19th century there are a number of reports of illegal gambling at the Vine. In July 1888 the landlord, William Bailey, was accused of allowing two men to 'toss for a cigar'. The loser then paid the landlord two-pence for a cigar. When called to give evidence, the landlord and a farmer named William Webster not only denied the charge but also alleged that the constables were drunk at the time. Not surprisingly, the landlord was found guilty and fined 20s and costs of 26s. 40 years later, another landlord was more fortunate.

According to a report in *The Derby Daily Telegraph* Sergeant Hutchinson of the Belper Police visited the Vine disguised as a farm labourer and he observed a number of men playing cribbage for money. At the end of each game the losers paid for the winners' beer. When questioned, the landlord, Ernest Hemmingway, appeared surprised and said he knew the men were playing cribbage but was not aware that they were playing for cash. On this occasion the magistrates gave him the benefit of the doubt and dismissed the case! It seems that the regulars at the Vine were a generous bunch and there are a number of reports of charitable collections and donations. One of the earliest of these was in November 1900 when 15 shillings was collected for the Derbyshire Transvaal War Fund. During the 1920s and 1930s the pub organised excursions to the seaside and other places of interest. In September 1929 *The Derbyshire Advertiser and Journal* reported that 'Members of the Vine (Mickleover) Outing Club journeyed to Liverpool on Monday and also visited New Brighton where an enjoyable time was spent'. In 1933 the destination was Blackpool when 20 'excursionists' presented the hostess, Mrs Hemmingway, with a pair of oxidised vases in thanks for 'an enjoyable day'. In recent years the Vine has had an uneventful history. Although refurbished a few years ago, it retains three separate cosy rooms and remains a popular local pub.

The Wagon and Horses on Ashbourne Road, Derby, was built in 1833. It was named from its use as a despatching point for fly wagons to points along the Ashbourne Turnpike, the tollgate for which was nearby. The Derby and County Athletics Club established their headquarters and held many of their presentations and social events here. In December 1897 the Wagon and Horses hosted a smoking concert where cross-country championship medals and other prizes were presented. Other sporting clubs also used the pub as a base or a starting point for their activities. In November 1889 the Derby Harriers held an eight-mile handicap starting from the Wagon and Horses. This was a 'hare and hounds' race that followed a course which included Mackworth, Vicar Wood and Markeaton. The pub was also used for the usual range of activities including sales, auctions and a variety of entertainment. Inquests were held here but unusually in 1880 three inquests were held here in less than a week. The causes of death were recorded as a rupture of a blood vessel in the brain and two cases of a rupture of a blood vessel in the heart. The pub continued to be a vital part of the local community throughout the 20th century and remains so today.

The Water Wheel at Hartshorne in South Derbyshire was originally a screw mill. In 1796 the mill employed 59 people, many of whom, according to a contemporary account, 'make an average 1,200 gross screws per week by means of 36 engines or lathes turned by one water wheel'. It was still in operation in the 1840s but was abandoned shortly afterwards. It was subsequently used partly as a sawmill and partly as a maltings. It lay derelict for some time but was eventually converted into a pub and restaurant.

The Waterfall, Derby.

The Waterfall on Railway Terrace in Derby was previously the Railway Institute. This was built in 1892 by the Midland Railway company as a cultural centre for its employees. It had a library, coffee room, classrooms, lecture and concert hall and other rooms for recreation and reading. The library closed in 1963 and its books were either sold or given away to members. The building was leased to the Post Office Social Club in the 1980s but that closed in 1994. After a period lying derelict it was opened as a pub in 1996.

The White Hart in Duffield dates from at least the latter years of the 18th century. Originally a small stone building with a thatched roof, it was for many years an important feature of the village. It is believed that Manorial courts were held here for a number of years. A contemporary account also records that a meeting of the local Militia Company was held there in 1798. The increased traffic through Duffield caused by the opening of the Duffield to Idridghay Turnpike around 1810 led to an extension being built at the front of the building. Stables and a forge were constructed at the rear of the building to provide for the travellers' horses. By the 19th century the inn provided a venue for a number of social events. A number of concerts were held there in 1835 and 1836. A Grand Miscellaneous Concert was held here on Tuesday, 10 May 1836. The patrons included the Hon Nathaniel Curzon and the Rev William Barber. The programme included works by Rossini and Haydn, with tickets priced at three

The White Hart, Duffield.

shillings. This was a considerable sum at the time and was probably justified by the fact that the publicity for the concert made it clear that it was aimed at 'the nobility, gentry and clergy of Duffield and its neighbourhood'. The Loyal Colville lodge of the Oddfellows friendly society held its meetings at the White Hart and in 1892 a Freemasons Lodge was dedicated in the village, being named the Ecclesbourne Lodge. Consecration took place at the Endowed schoolroom and afterwards the brethren dined at the White Hart. By the end of the 19th century the inn hosted meetings of a number of local societies, and in 1900 the landlord was granted licence extensions for the annual Dinners of the Cricket Club, Duffield Flower Show Committee, Duffield Horticultural Society, Masonic Banquet for the Ecclesbourne Lodge and the Duffield Angling Club. The hotel was rebuilt in 1937-38 behind the old premises and the new premises were opened in May 1938. The hotel continued to play a vital role in the life of the village, and in 1941 it was designated as the headquarters of the Duffield Home Guard. It remains a popular pub/restaurant which attracts customers from Duffield and the surrounding area.

The White Hart in Aston on Trent can be traced back to 1771 when it was owned by Christopher Wright. It remained in the same family until 1866 when it was sold to Edward Holden for £900. In a small village such as Aston, the landlord of the local inn was often a person of some substance and some importance. Mr Frank Ludlow became landlord of the White Hart towards the end of the 18th century. He lived in Aston for most of his life and filled most of the public offices there at one time or another. Amongst other things, he was a member of the Parish Council, a manager of the schools, a churchwarden and secretary and treasurer of the local friendly society, whilst for many years he was a member, and sometime chairman, of the Shardlow Board of Guardians For many years the White Hart played an important role in the life of the village and hosted many social and business functions. The local landowner collected his rents here and customarily treated his tenants to a dinner. In December 1910 *The Derbyshire Advertiser and Journal* reported that 'Major Winterbottom held his Michaelmas rent audit for his tenants in Aston, Shardlow and Wilne at the White

The White Hart, Aston on Trent.

Hart. The attendance was very fair, and after an excellent dinner ... the remainder of the evening was spent in speeches and songs'. In 1919, following the end of World War One, a 'farewell' smoking concert was given to the 'volunteers' of Aston and the neighbouring villages. The band and concert party of the Derby branch of the Discharged Soldiers Federation enlivened the proceedings and toasts were drunk to the King and the officers of the old battalion. In the same year the local branch of the Conservative and Unionist Association held a successful function here, which included 'vocal and instrumental items' as well as humorous selections and speeches on current politics. Sales of land and property were held at the White Hart and the Aston on Trent Cricket Club held their annual dinners there. Little is known of the pub in the latter years of the 20th century and it received little attention in the local press. It remains the centre of village life and both the Aston and Weston branch of the Royal British Legion and the Aston on Trent Local History Group both hold their meetings here.

The White Horse in the Morledge, Derby, was originally one of a line of three small inns: the Noah's Ark, the Cossack and the White Horse. Pountains acquired the White Horse and the Cossack and proceeded to demolish them both in 1920. In their place a new larger and lavishly decorated White Horse was built, which was formally opened in 1925. The completion and opening of the hotel and restaurant was marked by a luncheon held in the restaurant on Friday, 10 July. This was attended by friends and well-wishers, including Mr R N Saxton, the Chairman of Pountains, Mr T

The White Horse, Derby.

H Thorpe, the Architect, and the Mayor, Councillor A Mycroft. Trade may have been slow to develop as a notice was placed in *The Derby Daily Telegraph* describing the hotel as 'one of the latest and best furnished in Derby' with 'splendid accommodation for smoking concerts, meetings, parties, dinners etc' and 'up-to-date catering'. Over the next three decades the White Horse was the venue of choice for dozens of different organisations, including old comrade's groups, trade unions, trade associations and a wide range of sporting clubs and associations. This latter group included Derbyshire Amateurs FC, Old Derbeans Football Club, Derby Cyclists Touring Club, Derby Cables Ltd Fishing Club, Derbyshire County Hockey Association and Derby Amateur Boxing Club. Retirement presentations were frequently held there. In the 1960s musicians and 'pop stars' performing in Derby often stayed at the White Horse. These included Cliff Richard, who was a guest here in 1960. In recent years it has been known by a number of names including the Court House and the Foal and Ferkin. Today it is a popular town-centre pub, well known for its live music.

The White Horse at Stanton in South Derbyshire is the oldest pub in the village and may date from the 17th century. A document of 1786 described the inn as having a barn, stables, outhouses and a garden. According to some accounts, it was previously

The White Swan, Littleover.

known as the Eagle & Sun. It is not known when the pub changed its name, but in 1820 John Orgill was recorded as being the landlord of the White Horse. The pub played an important part in the social life of the village for many years. The land behind the club was the home ground for Stanton Cricket Club and it also hosted cricket and quoits clubs. The quoits club were undefeated champions of Burton and District Association, Second Division in 1901.

The White Swan on Shepherd Street, Littleover, is believed to date from the 18th century. Little is known about its early history but the area around the pub was originally the heart of the village where significant social gatherings would have taken place. In 1879 it was described as comprising a bar, club room, tap room, kitchen, good cellar, two bedrooms, stable large garden and outhouses. The pages of the local newspapers record auctions, inquests and a variety of social functions being held here. It seems to have been a rather unruly house in the latter years of the 19th century and there are various reports in the local press of drunkenness and disorderly behaviour. When such cases were brought before the magistrates, they usually resulted in the imposition of a small fine. Misbehaviour on the part of the landlord was, however, a more serious affair. In July 1883 Henry Spencer, the landlord of the White Swan, was convicted of having refused to admit police-constable Turner to his premises. He was fined 10s and costs but when the renewal of his licence was considered a few months later, the police objected. He was fortunate as the bench merely cautioned him and allowed the renewal of his licence. History repeated itself in the 20th century for in 1940 the landlord found himself on a blacklist and his licence was renewed only provisionally. This restriction was lifted only a few months later so it appears that during this period of time the landlord behaved himself! In other respects, the White Swan appears to have been a respectable pub. In March 1924 the Buffalos (a friendly society) opened a new lodge at the White Swan when, according to *The Derby Daily Telegraph*, 'a large gathering assembled ... to witness the opening of a new lodge to be named the Ivy Lodge. Many lodges sent representatives ... Ten new members were initiated and many others affiliated to the Lodge'. In the period before the founding of the NHS, the Derby Royal Infirmary depended on voluntary contributions. Various collections were made at the White Swan. In March 1941, for example, £3 1s was collected for the Infirmary Building Fund. The White Swan remains a popular community-based pub that attracts local people with a wide range of drinks and home-cooked food.

WHAT'S IN A NAME

The Abbey in Darley Abbey was once part of an Augustinian abbey. The building of the abbey church was completed in 1146 and was dedicated to the Virgin Mary. Over the next few years other buildings were added including cloisters, refectory, dormitories, chapter house and guest house as well as various outbuildings such as the kitchen, brewhouse, bake-house, barns and workshops. It received endowments of land as well as other gifts from benefactors and became a very wealthy community. Like other abbeys throughout the kingdom, it was closed on the orders of King Henry VIII. The buildings were torn down and eventually little trace remained. The building that became the Abbey Pub survived but eventually fell into disrepair. It lay derelict for a number of years but became a pub in 1980.

The Arkwright Arms at Chesterfield takes its name from the famous family of that name. According to some accounts the pub was once owned by William Arkwright, a descendant of the famous Richard Arkwright, the inventor of the spinning frame and the man responsible for building the world's first cotton mill at Cromford in 1771.

Born in Preston in 1732, Richard Arkwright became a travelling barber and wigmaker, which brought him into contact with families engaged in spinning and weaving. Building on the ideas of others, he succeeded in constructing a prototype roller spinning machine which could be operated by an unskilled worker and was capable of being linked to an external source of power. He moved to Nottingham in 1786 and entered into partnership with two wealthy stocking manufacturers, Samuel Need and Jedediah Strutt. They financed the construction of a cotton mill in Nottingham which was driven by horse power. When this was successful, they decided to build a much larger water-powered cotton mill at Cromford in Derbyshire. This

The Abbey Pub Sign. The Abbey Pub was originally part of Darley Abbey and may have been the guest house.

opened in 1771 and was a considerable commercial and technological success. Following his success at Cromford, Arkwright went on to build more mills, either with others or independently. All were driven by water and operated according to the same system which he had perfected in his original mill at Cromford. His empire continued to grow and he began to amass a huge fortune. With wealth came enhanced social standing and in 1787 he was appointed High Sheriff of Derbyshire and shortly afterwards was knighted by King George III. He died on 3 August 1792, aged 60. He changed forever the way in which we work and the historian David Jeremy recently declared: 'The Arkwright system substituted capital for labour, machines for skill, factory for home and mill discipline for family work routines'. Considering the significance of his achievements, it is surprising that so few pubs bear his name.

The Babington Arms in Green Lane, Derby, is a modern pub which is part of the Weatherspoon's chain. It was built on land that was once part of the gardens of the long-demolished Babington House. This 17th-century mansion was the home of the Babington family, whose coat of arms depicted two baboons on a large beer or wine cask. Anthony Babington was hanged, drawn and quartered in September 1586 because of his involvement in a plot to assassinate Queen Elizabeth I and place Mary, Queen of Scots, on the throne.

The Bentley Brook Inn takes is name from the Bentley Brook, a stream that runs close to the pub. It is a small tributary of the River Dove and is 11.5 km in length. From its source near Brassington, it flows through Bradbourne and Fenny Bentley.

The Bentley Brook Inn.

After passing to the north of Ashbourne, it joins the River Dove near the village of Mayfield. In the 18th century it was used to power a cotton mill at Bradbourne and a corn mill near Fenny Bentley.

The Black Diamond is a modern pub in Creswell. Coal was mined here until the pit closed in 1991 and the pub was situated only about 500 yards from the colliery gate. Its name is a reference to the coal mining heritage of the area and the wealth and prosperity that was formerly derived from its presence. At one time the phrase 'a black diamond' referred to what might be called 'a rough diamond' today; someone of good moral quality but unpolished manners. Perhaps an appropriate epithet for a Derbyshire coal miner!

The Boat Inn at Cromford has an unusual name for a pub so far from the sea. It was built around 1772 as a flour merchant's business, but by the early 1830s it was being used as a beer house and was known as the New Inn. The first known landlord was Anthony Boden, who was also a butcher. Later the name was changed to the Hit and Miss. By 1835 it belonged to William Allen, who was a boatman on the Cromford Canal. He changed the name to the Boat Inn and it has remained so for almost two centuries.

The Bonnie Prince at Chellaston, near Derby, takes its name from Bonnie Prince Charlie who led a rebellion in 1745 in an attempt to seize the throne from George III. The advance guard of his army reached as far as Swarkestone Bridge, only a short distance from this modern pub. The main army only got as far as Derby when the Prince, much against his wishes, was persuaded to abandon his march on London

The Boat Inn, Cromford.

Mural on the side of the Boat Inn.

Statue of Bonnie Prince Charlie on Cathedral Green, Derby.

and return to Scotland. A statue on Cathedral Green, Derby, depicts the Prince looking over his shoulder as he begins his retreat.

The Brick and Tile on Brick Street, Derby, was built in the first half of the 18th century but has been much altered since. It has been suggested that its name was taken from the brickyard that flourished there at that time.

The Bubble Inn on the Trent and Mersey Canal at Stenson (a suburb of Derby) is housed in a converted 19th-century farm building. It takes its name from the Stenson Bubble, an unusual feature which causes the water to bubble when re-entering the canal below the lock.

The Butterley Park at Codnor takes its name from the famous Butterley Engineering Company. This was founded in 1790 by Benjamin Outram and Francis Beresford to mine coal and iron on the Butterley Hall estate. The company expanded rapidly and only a year later the partnership was extended to include the canal engineer William Jessop and the Nottingham banker Joseph Wright. The works was developed and expanded to take advantage of the increased demand for pig iron. Work on a new iron works at Codnor Park commenced in 1810 and involved the construction of blast furnaces, forges, lime kilns and dwelling houses. A company village (Ironville) was built between 1834 and 1843. When completed, it comprised 120 solidly built houses as well as shops, church, school, mechanics' institute and sports ground. The settlement was also provided with its own gas and water works and even had its own newspaper, *The Ironville Telegraph*. In its heyday the company produced a huge variety of cast-iron goods. These included munitions, pipes and other equipment for gas and water works, along with rails and structural ironwork for bridges and buildings. The Butterley company achieved a national and international reputation but is perhaps best known for the ironwork for the roof of St Pancras Railway Station.

The Canal Turn at Spondon was until recently known as the Moon Inn. Its history can be traced back to the Canal Tavern which was built shortly after the opening of the nearby Derby Canal. This was renamed the Station Inn with the coming of the railway. This was in turn demolished in 1929 and replaced by the Moon just 30 yards away. It underwent a major overhaul in 2016 when it was relaunched as a restaurant and sports bar.

The Castle Hotel in Hatton takes its name from the nearby Tutbury Castle which it overlooks. Tutbury Castle is perhaps best known as one of the prisons of Mary, Queen of Scots. Considerable work was done to prepare apartments for her incarceration, but she was unhappy there and wrote to Queen Elizabeth complaining that, 'this damp and uninhabited house has given me a cold and a headache'. Tutbury Castle is in the care of the Duchy of Lancaster and is open to the public.

The Castle Hotel in Castleton is another public house which owes its name to the proximity of a castle. Peveril Castle, which overlooks the town, was built by William Peverel, one of William the Conqueror's most trusted knights. Its purpose was to protect Peak Forest, an area rich in lead. The Kings of England were frequent visitors to the castle during the Middle Ages. On occasions it was used as a royal hunting lodge as it lay within the Royal Forest of the Peak and the area provided rich sport for the Plantagenet kings who were able to hunt wolves, wild boar and deer there. The 14th century was a turbulent time and the castle changed hands on several occasions during this time. It eventually became part of the Duchy of Lancaster, but by this time it had ceased to have any importance either as a fortification or a residence. Before long the hall and other buildings were dismantled in order to use the building materials. In 1561 its demolition was considered but rejected on the grounds that the keep served 'for the keeping of the Courts' while the bailey was useful for impounding stray cattle. In 1609 a survey of 'decayed castells' declared that Peverel Castle was 'very ruinous and served for noe use'. Today the castle is in the care of English Heritage and is open to the public.

The Castle Inn at Bakewell is a traditional inn which was built in the 16th century. Its name is derived from a small motte and bailey castle, probably dating from the 12th century and standing on the eastern side of Bakewell overlooking the town and the river. It was razed to the ground as a consequence of the English Civil War and now only the earthworks survive. In the 10th century a fort was also built here on the orders of King Edward the Elder. Local tradition suggests that it may have been built on Castle Hill.

The Cat and Fiddle at Kirk Hallam is a modern estate pub which takes its name from the nearby Cat and Fiddle windmill. This was constructed around 1788 and is one of the finest post mills in the country. For many years it was owned by British Steel who maintained it in good condition. It is now in private ownership and is not open to the public.

The Cavendish Hotel at Baslow is an 18th-century village inn and was originally known as

Cat and Fiddle Pub sign.

the Peacock. It is located on the Chatsworth Estate and passed into the ownership of the Cavendish family in 1830. Sir William Cavendish was the second husband of the famous Bess of Hardwick who built Hardwick Hall. In 1694 another William Cavendish was created Duke of Devonshire as a reward for his support of William and Mary during the Glorious Revolution. The Cavendish Hotel is now part of the Devonshire Hotels and Restaurants Group which is owned by the Duke and Duchess of Devonshire.

The Charles Cotton Hotel in Hartington dates from the early 17th century. It takes its name from the famous author, angler and friend of Izaak Walton. He lived at Beresford Hall and enjoyed fly fishing on the River Dove. He contributed sections on fly fishing and the making of artificial flies to the fifth edition of *The Complete Angler*.

The Cheshire Cheese Inn on the outskirts of Hope was so named because it was an overnight stop on the old trade route from Cheshire. Packhorse trains stopped here and it is said that payment for lodging was actually paid in cheese!

The Chip and Pin is a micro-pub in Melbourne which was opened in 2014. Its name reflects the fact that the building was previously a branch of HSBC Bank. The side room, which was previously the bank manager's office, contains a splendid table and chairs and is available for meetings, with a serving hatch through to the cask room where the beer is kept. There is no traditional bar in the pub but a friendly and efficient 'table service' is provided.

The Coates Park Inn at Somercotes was built in the 1960s and takes its name from the nearby industrial estate. This comprises a range of warehouse, industrial and office premises within a fenced and gated site. It is located close to the centre of Alfreton and provides easy access to the M1.

The Chip and Pin, Melbourne.

The Cock Inn at Mugginton was once known as the Cock Horse Inn. In the 18th and 19th centuries the turnpike road outside the inn formed part of the important route from London to Manchester and was built near the summit of a long hill from Weston Underwood. As well as being an inn and a tollbar, the pub also hired out cock horses. These were strong animals capable of helping heavy wagons make it to the top of the hill. The stables housing these horses were demolished in the 1960s but previously stood on the site of the present pub restaurant. At some point in the past the Cock Horse Inn became the Cock Inn and the origin of the name was lost. The inn ceased trading in 2006 and lay semi-derelict for some time. It was restored and reopened in 2017.

The Cock and Magpie at Old Whittington, Chesterfield, is located adjacent to Revolution House. This was previously the Cock and Pynot (on old-fashioned dialect term for a magpie) alehouse where in 1688 three noblemen plotted to overthrow King James II and replace him with William and Mary of Orange, an event

The Cock and Magpie Inn sign.

The Cock and Magpie.

known as the Glorious Revolution. The Cock and Magpie also appear on the coat of arms of Chesterfield.

The Cock and Pullet Inn at Sheldon near Bakewell was opened in 1995. It was once a farm building and takes its name from the cockerels and pullets which used to run around in front of the barn where the pub is now situated. The village's previous pub, The Devonshire Arms, which stood next door, is now a private house.

The Coronation at Crewton in Derby was planned in 1937, the year of George VI's coronation, and completed in 1939. George VI succeeded to the throne following the abdication of his brother King Edward VIII. He played an important morale-boosting role during World War Two and made a secret visit to Derby on 8 August 1940 when he toured the Rolls-Royce works and inspected Indian troops camped near Ashbourne. He was the last Emperor of India and the first Head of the Commonwealth. He died in 1952 and was succeeded by his daughter Queen Elizabeth II.

The Crewe and Harpur at Swarkestone takes its names from two prominent local families who were eventually united in marriage. Their seat was at Calke Abbey in Derbyshire. They were in many ways a rather eccentric family. Sir Henry Harpur was something of a recluse but caused a scandal by marrying his mistress, a ladies maid at Calke. The 10th Baronet Sir Vauncey Harpur Crewe served as High Sheriff of Derbyshire in 1900 but apart from this played no part in public life. He shunned modern trappings and motor cars and even bicycles were banned from the estate. His

The Crewe and Harpur at Swarkestone.

passion was for collecting stuffed animals and birds and when he died in 1924 there were several hundred specimens in the house. The baronetcy became extinct upon his death and in 1985 Calke Abbey passed into the ownership of the National Trust.

The Cross Daggers pub at Coal Aston near Dronfield lies just a few miles south of Sheffield and may refer to the badge of the Hallamshire Cutlers Company. This is a trade guild of metalworkers based in Sheffield. It was incorporated by an Act of Parliament in 1624 which gave the company jurisdiction over 'all persons using to make Knives, Blades, Scissors, Sheeres, Sickles, and all other wares and manufacture made or wrought of yron and steele, dwelling or inhabiting within six miles compasse of the same'. The company still exists today and from its headquarters at Cutlers Hall in Sheffield it continues to promote and support the industries and businesses of the area.

The Crown and Arrows is a modern pub in the Shelton Lock area of Derby. It lies adjacent to St Edmunds Church and it is from this that the pub derives its name. Saint Edmund, the last King of the East Angles, was killed in 870 by the Danes. After refusing to renounce Christ, the Danes beat him, shot him with arrows and then beheaded him on the orders of Ivar the Boneless. St Edmund's emblem is a crown and arrows, hence the name of the pub.

The Derby Tup on the outskirts of Chesterfield takes its name from a mumming play traditionally performed during the Christmas and New Year period in parts of

North Derbyshire. The Tup itself comprises a head on a pole with snapping jaws and ram's horns. This is held by an operator, hidden under a sackcloth, to represent the body of the creature. The performance is accompanied by the singing of the traditional folk song *The Derby Ram* in which a gigantic beast is slaughtered to provide amazing items for the townsfolk of Derby. Other characters in the play include the Tup's keeper, Beelzebub and Little Devil Doubt. The tradition survived well into the 20th century and by the 1970s over 40 Old Tup troupes were recorded as performing in North East Derbyshire. One historian has described it as 'the most noteworthy example of continuously performed regional folk-drama in Britain'.

The Devonshire Arms at Beeley is situated on the Chatsworth estate, with Chatsworth House, the home of the Dukes of Devonshire, only a short drive away. It was opened in 1747 when three cottages were converted into an inn. It was for many years a coaching inn on the route from London. Its many famous visitors included Charles Dickens, the famous Victorian novelist. It has been rumoured that King Edward VII met his mistress Alice Keppel here on a number of occasions. It is today part of the Devonshire Hotels and Restaurants Group which is owned by the Duke and Duchess of Devonshire. Other properties in the group include the Cavendish Hotel at Baslow and the Devonshire Arms at Pilsley.

The Erewash Hotel on Station Road, Ilkeston, takes its name from the River Erewash which marks the boundary between Derbyshire and Nottinghamshire for much of its length. From its source near Kirkby-in-Ashfield in Nottinghamshire, it flows westwards

The Five Lamps, Derby.

to Eastwood and then south through Ilkeston and Sandiacre before joining the River Trent near Long Eaton. The river also gives its name to Erewash Borough Council, which was formed in 1974 when the former borough of Ilkeston and the urban district of Long Eaton were united with some of the surrounding rural areas.

The Five Lamps pub in Derby was previously known as the Saint Helen's Inn, which was built around 1850 and was itself originally known as the New Inn. The original building was demolished and replaced with the present structure in the 1930s. Its

The Flower Pot, Derby.

present name is derived from the iconic five lamps which previously stood close to the pub and after which the local area was also named. It closed for a period but reopened in 2011 and is now a popular and flourishing real ale pub.

The Flower Pot stands on the corner of King Street and Chapel Street, Derby. It dates from the early years of the 18th century and was originally a private residence. The origin of the name relates to the flower shows which for many years were held in the nearby Drill Hall.

The Flying Childers at Stanton in the Peak is named after a famous undefeated thoroughbred race horse of the 18th century. The horse gained its name from his breeder, Colonel Leonard Childers, as well as the owner, the Duke of Devonshire. He was known variously as Devonshire Childers or Flying Childers or sometimes simply as Childers. Although the Duke received many offers for the colt, including one to pay for the horse's weight in gold, he remained the animal's owner throughout its life. According to some accounts the pub acquired its name when a previous landlord won a considerable amount of money by backing the horse.

The Friary in Friar Gate, Derby, takes its name from the Dominican Friary which once stood on the site. The Dominicans were an order of friar preachers whose aim was to go out into the world to help the poor and the sick and to spread the work of God by means of homely and vigorous preaching. They were popular with ordinary people and attracted both recruits and benefactions. The friars, who numbered about 30 in Derby,

The Friary Hotel, Derby.

went quietly about their work for over three centuries. Preaching in the market place and in local churches, they attracted large congregations and, when they first arrived, they brought about something of a religious revival. Following the Reformation, the Friary was surrendered to the Crown. The present building was constructed in 1731 as a town house for Samuel Crompton. The building was extended in 1760 and again in

The Great Northern, Mickleover.

The Grouse and Claret, Rowsley.

1875. It was purchased by the Whitaker family in 1922, who soon set about converting the building into a licensed hotel. Beer was brewed on the premises for a short period during the 1930s. It has been extended on a number of occasions but has had a chequered history in recent decades. It has recently been described as a 'studenty pub'!

The Great Northern on Station Road, Mickleover, takes its name from the Great Northern Railway which once ran next to it. It was opened in 1876 around the same time that the railway company built an extension from Friargate station in Derby as far as Egginton Junction. Although the railway line closed in 1968, it continued to be used by the British Rail research department to test model trains for the future Channel Tunnel.

The Grouse and Claret at Rowsley was previously the Station Hotel and was built to serve the needs of passengers alighting at the nearby railway station (now part of the Peak Shopping Village). Its present name comes from a type of artificial fly used by fly fishermen on the River Derwent which flows through Chatsworth and Rowsley. According to some accounts it was a favourite of the local water bailiff.

The Hardinge Arms at Kings Newton dates back to the 16th century but only became a public house much later. By the middle of the 19th century the premises comprised a house, stable, cow shed, timber shed, wheelwright's shop and garden. The owner at that time, Thomas Taft, was a wheelwright but the building was later converted to a beer shop and then a public house run by Mrs Eleanor Stafford. The pub takes the name from the Hardinge family of nearby Kings Newton Hall. They were squires here for over 300 years and supported the King during the Civil War. The arms displayed on the pub sign are those of Viscount Hardinge which were granted to the family after they had left King's Newton. The detached function room of the pub was demolished a few years ago to make way for a small estate of private houses.

The Hardinge Arms sign.

The Harrington Arms at Thurlston takes its name from the family that lived at nearby Elvaston Castle. For several generations the Earls of Harrington served as Members of Parliament and senior army officers. The fourth Earl caused a scandal by marrying Maria Foote, an actress 17 years his junior. They were described by a contemporary as 'a besotted and inseparable

The Harrington Arms, Thurlston.

The Honeycomb Pub, Mickleover.

couple'. Following the Countryside Act 1968, the 11th Earl Harrington sold the estate to Derbyshire County Council in 1969.

The Honeycomb pub on Ladybank Road, Mickleover, opened on 1 November 1974 to serve the newly built Ladybank Estate. Its name is derived from its unusual hexagonal room structure. As well as the usual brewery officials and local councillors, the opening ceremony was also attended by representatives of the Derbyshire Bee Keepers Association.

The Hunters Arms at Kilburn was built in 1879. It takes its name from the Hunter family who owned Kilburn Hall, and virtually the whole village for around 200 years, until 1890. It closed for a short period but was reopened in 2009. It has since won the Amber Valley CAMRA Pub of the Year award on more than one occasion.

The James Wyatt at Alvaston is named after the architect who designed the nearby Elvaston Castle. The original manor house was built in the early 17th century but it was redesigned and extended in the early years of the 19th century. Wyatt was

The Honeycomb Pub sign.

responsible for the new wing, a great hall and most of the lavish gothic interiors of the castle. Unfortunately he died in 1813 before the work was completed.

The Jessop Arms is in Jessop Street, Codnor. The street and the pub both take their name from William Jessop (the younger) who together with his brother George Jessop and another partner, William Needham, formed the Ironville Benefit Building Society. This was instrumental in building a new estate of houses which was scheduled to be called Codnorville. Three new streets were named after the partners of the Butterley Company: Wright Street, Needham Street and Jessop Street.

The Jodrell Arms at Whaley Bridge commemorates the Jodrell family who were major landowners in the area from the 13th century. Roger Jodrell was one of King Henry V's archers at the Battle of Agincourt. The family is also remembered by the Jodrell Bank radio telescope The Jodrell Arms is a Grade II listed building. It was closed at the time of writing and has been awaiting the completion of refurbishment work for some years.

The John Thomson at Ingleby was the first (and possibly the only) pub to be named after its owner. In 1968 John and Ann Thompson converted their 15th century farmhouse into what is now known as the John Thompson Inn & Brewery. Only nine years later it won the coveted Pub of the Year trophy and is one of only eight pubs in the whole of the country to have been recommended in each and every annual edition of *The Good Pub Guide*. A micro-brewery was added to the business and in 1977 the first pint of JTS XXX was pulled to celebrate the Queen's Silver Jubilee.

The King Alfred pub in Alfreton is a substantial mock Tudor building believed to have been constructed in the 1930s. At first glance the name does not appear to have any local significance. It was, however, believed by many people that the town derived its name from Alfred's Tun or Alfred's Town, hence the pub name. More recent research, however, indicates that although the place name is of Saxon origin the town does not have any relationship with King Alfred.

The Knockerdown Inn near Ashbourne overlooks the southern end of Carsington Water. The building dates back to the 17th century but it is believed that it opened as a tavern in 1838. According to some accounts, the unusual name is linked to the lead mining industry and is believed to relate to knocking lead and limestone from the roof of a shaft. It is perhaps also noteworthy that according to local folklore a 'knocker' is a sort of goblin that inhabits lead mines.

The Lantern Pike in Little Hayfield is probably unique as a pub name as it takes its name from the hill at the back of the pub. The hill lies within the Peak District National Park and is 373 metres high. It is believed that the name derives from its use as a beacon for communication in bye-gone days. It is a popular hiking destination and is often considered a continuation of the nearby Kinder

Scout. The Lantern Pike Dash, a fell race, is held here in May each year. In 1927 the landlady of the inn was murdered for just the £40 takings in a tin. The lead pipe used to kill her was later found in the toilet cistern.

The Larklands is an estate pub that was built to serve the Larklands area of Ilkeston. Larklands Avenue and some of the neighbouring streets were built on an area formerly known as the Lark and Capon Lands.

The Last Post in the Rowditch area of Derby is a micro-pub that was opened in 2015. It was previously the local post office where people went to collect their pensions, buy stamps and send parcels.

The Lime Kiln Pub sign.

The Lime Kiln on Cromford Road, Wirksworth, takes its name from the limestone quarrying and lime burning which was an important part of the local economy for over two centuries. Lime kilns were used in the 18th and 19th centuries to create quicklime.

The Lime Kiln Pub at Wirksworth.

The Lock Keepers Rest, Sawley.

This was used for improving the quality of agricultural land, as well as for mortar and limewash. In addition, it was also used for a wide range of small-scale industrial purposes such as tanning, textiles, soap and papermaking that took place in Wirksworth and other settlements in the area.

The Little Castle at Duckmanton is a modern, family-friendly pub. The name is a reference to the Little Castle (part of Bolsover Castle) less than three miles away. The Little Castle was constructed in the early 17th century and contains some lavishly decorated rooms. These include the Elysium Chamber (which depicts the gods and goddesses of Ancient Greece), the Star Chamber and the Hall where a series of paintings depict the labours of Hercules. Bolsover Castle is in the care of English Heritage and is open to the public.

The Lock Keepers Rest is a micro-pub at Sawley Lock near Long Eaton. Dave Parrot, the last paid keeper at Sawley Locks, was allowed to buy the cottage when he retired in 2014. He renovated the building and later turned part of it into the Lock Keepers Rest micro-pub. It serves real ale and has room for about 12 inside with more seating outside. It's open Thursday evening to Sunday lunchtime. According to the local branch of CAMRA, there are four changing beers on gravity.

The Manifold Inn is a 200-year-old coaching inn near Hartington. It lies within its own grounds nestling on the banks of the River Manifold and it is from this that it takes its name.

The Markham Arms at Brimington near Chesterfield takes its name from the Markham family who lived at Tapton Hall. Charles Paxton Markham was an industrialist with interests in both coalmining and engineering. He showed a deep concern for the welfare of his employees. A generous philanthropist, he financed open-air swimming baths, hospital wards, a refuge for homeless men and a rest home for former employees. He was also a member of Chesterfield Corporation for 25 years and mayor on three occasions. His sister Violet Markham was a writer, social reformer and campaigner against women's suffrage. Her primary interest was in education and she was a member of Chesterfield Education Authority from 1899 to 1934. Like her brother, she also served as Mayor of Chesterfield. The Markham Arms was recently refurbished and is currently part of the Admiral Taverns group of pubs.

The Marquis of Ormonde at Codnor-Denby Lane, Ripley, has a rather obscure connection with the coal mining heritage of the area. Walter Butler became the Marquis of Ormonde in 1815. Through marriage he inherited the mining rights in Codnor and Loscoe. These mining rights were later purchased by the Butterley Company who sunk the Ormonde Fields Colliery in 1906. It closed in September 1970.

The Melbourne Arms at Melbourne was previously known as the Lamb Inn. It is named after William Lamb (Lord Melbourne) of Melbourne Hall who was a British Prime Minister during the reign of Queen Victoria. In his earlier life he was also the husband of the notorious Lady Caroline Lamb who had an infamous affair with Lord Byron. It was she who described him as 'Mad, bad and dangerous to know'.

The Merlin on Pride Park, Derby, is a modern pub and part of the Hungry Horse chain. It takes its name from the Merlin aero engine manufactured by Rolls-Royce. This famous engine with its distinctive roar powered the Spitfires and Hurricanes that defended this country in the Battle of Britain. It was formerly called by the less exciting name of the Pride Park.

The Merry Widows stands on the corner of Railway Terrace and Midland Place, close to the railway station in Derby. It was built around 1890 and was previously named Wright's Vaults after its founder. For many years it was known locally as

The Merry Widows Pub sign.

The Merry Widows, Derby.

the 'Merry Widow's' after a notable landlady of very many years ago. It was renamed the Merry Widows in 1992. The present pub sign shows two stylishly dressed ladies of an uncertain age who look as though they might be about to catch the train for a day's shopping!

The Midway pub was built in 1964 on the site of the Lower Midway pottery. Its licence was transferred from the Victoria Inn, Church Greasley, when it was demolished in the same year. The pub obviously takes its name from the district in which it is located. Between 1906 and 1927 the Burton and Ashby Light Railway (a tramway system) operated between these two towns. The tram sheds at Midway were roughly mid-way between these two places.

The Mile in Friargate, Derby, takes its name from a famous pub crawl whose route lay along the length of Friargate and beyond. Originally this commenced at the Derbyshire Yeoman and ended at the Lord Nelson in the Wardwick. Several of the pubs on the route have since been demolished or have changed their use.

The Millhouse at Milford takes its name from the mills which were built here in the 1780s. The mill complex eventually included spinning, bleaching and dying mills as well as foundries, joiners workshops, a gas works and a corn mill. Most of the early mills were demolished in the 1950s and 1960s, although the majority of the associated industrial housing has survived.

The Miner's Standard at Winster takes its name from the standard dish which was once used by lead miners to measure their ore. A standard dish made in 1512 is kept in the Moot Hall at Wirksworth. The village of Winster was an important lead mining centre for hundreds of years. The last local mine closed in 1938.

Mr Grundy's Tavern on Ashbourne Road, Derby, is named after Clifford Grundy, a veteran of World War One. Born in Derby in 1897, he enlisted in the Sherwood Foresters Regiment and was commissioned as a Second lieutenant. He survived the war and married Florence Aulton in 1923. A few years later the couple moved into the house at 36 Ashbourne Road adjacent to the Georgian House Hotel. When this house was converted into a pub the new owners decided to name it after the previous occupant and feature his image, in his regimental uniform, on the pub sign and promotional material. A Mr Grundy's brewery also operates on the site.

The Mundy Arms at Mackworth takes its name from the Mundy family who owned the Markeaton Hall Estate from 1516. John Mundy was a goldsmith who became Lord Mayor of London in 1522 and was knighted a few years later. The last member of the Mundy family to live at the hall was Francis Noel, who died in 1903. On the death of his wife 26 years later, the estate passed to the Rev William Clarke-Maxwell. In 1929 he gave the hall and 20 acres of its gardens to the Corporation on condition that the whole area would be used as a public park. The Mundy arms dates from the 16th century. It is part of the Chef and Brewer chain. The adjacent Premier Inn provides accommodation for travellers and visitors to the area.

The Mundy Arms at Marlpool near Heanor takes its name from the Miller Mundy family from nearby Shipley Hall (demolished in 1943). The family's wealth came from coal mining and in 1899 they were employing over 2,000 colliers at their Shipley pits and raising over 420,000 tons of coal annually. Alfred Edward Miller Mundy was the last Squire of Shipley and Mapperley to occupy Shipley Hall. He was a generous benefactor to both the local hospital and Cotmanhay Church, where many of his ancestors were buried. Following his death in 1922 the family sold Shipley Hall to the Shipley Colliery Company in which they were still shareholders. Eventually coal was mined underneath the hall and mining subsidence caused so much damage that the building became unsafe and had to be demolished. The Mundy Arms is a modern pub and part of the Hungry Horse chain.

The Navigation Inn at Breaston owes its name to its original proximity to the Derby Canal, whose route passed by the rear of the pub. There was a wharf here that enabled goods to be loaded and unloaded and also allowed barges to be turned around. This line of the canal linked Derby with the Erewash Canal at Sandiacre. In addition to coal, barges also carried a wide range of goods including corn, iron, limestone, paving stones and timber.

The Noah's Ark Pub, Derby.

The New Zealand Arms has no link with the Commonwealth country. It takes its name from the area in which it is located. This in turn was named after the farm on which the estate was constructed. It is believed that the farm adopted its name following the Treaty of Watangi, which was signed in 1840.

The Noah's Ark in the Morledge, Derby, takes its name from a famous criminal 'fence' and forger who lived on an Ark on the River Derwent near the centre of Derby. According to legend, Noah Bullock was finally exposed for his crimes in 1676 and

The Newdigate Arms, West Hallam.

appeared before the Recorder for Derby, Sir Simon Degg. It appears that he knew Degg well and promised to end his criminal activities and destroy his ark in order to escape the gallows. The Noah's Ark pub is thought to have been named after him and may be haunted by his ghost! The pub has been described as 'a real traditional boozer' which caters for 'an older generation of men and women who still like to have a good time and a bit of banter'.

The Newdigate Arms at West Hallam takes its name from the Newdigate family who lived at West Hallam Hall. They were lords of the manor and owned much of the land in the area. The family relinquished their interests in the village in 1914. The final Lord of the Manor was Sir Francis Newdigate. He was Governor of Tasmania (1917-1920) and of Western Australia (1920-24).

The Norfolk Arms in Glossop was once a Royal Mail coaching inn. Its name refers to the close relationship of the Dukes of Norfolk with the area. The town itself was built on land owned by the Norfolk family. The 13th Duke, Charles Henry Howard, built the market hall, railway station and the waterworks at Swineshaw that provided a piped supply of drinking water to the town. The Norfolk Arms is located in the historic Norfolk Square in the centre of the town. The original cobbled courtyard is now a beer garden.

The Oak and Acorn at Oakwood has an obvious connection to the modern suburb of Derby in which it is located. Oakwood was built mainly in the 1980s and

The Observatory, Ilkeston.

1990s and is one of the largest new housing estates in Europe, with a population of over 13,000. It was built on the site of an area of ancient oak woodland. Part of this has been preserved as Chaddesden Wood Nature Reserve. The Oak and Acorn is part of the Sizzling Pub chain. It features a dedicated darts alley and entertainment is provided by regular quiz nights.

The Observatory in Ilkeston is a Wetherspoons pub which was previously a small supermarket operated by the now defunct Safeway chain. The large front windows were retained in the conversion and allow customers to 'observe' the goings on in the town. There may also be a connection to the fact that John Flamstead, who became the first Astronomer Royal, was born at Denby, only a few miles away.

The Old Clubhouse in Buxton was previously the Union Club. This was built in 1886 and provided a venue for members of any of the well-known London gentlemen's clubs to use when they were visiting Buxton. When the club closed in 1969 the building was converted to become a public bar. The name is an obvious reference to its previous use.

The Ostrich Inn at Longford takes its name from the ostrich feathers which formed part of the crest of the Coke family who lived for many years at Longford Hall.

The Paper Mill at Darley Abbey is a single storey ex-British Legion Club which was rescued from unprofitability and sold to a local business by the trustees. Its name refers to the paper mill which was once part of the nearby mill complex, built by the Evans family in the 18th and 19th centuries. In the short time it has been open it has become a popular venue. According to CAMRA it serves two guest ales and a varying number of guest ciders.

The Pig of Lead at Bonsall refers to the lead mining heritage of the area. The Romans mined lead in Derbyshire and a number of pigs of lead have been discovered on Cromford Moor. An iconic stone figure of the 't'owd man' (a medieval representation of a lead miner) was discovered in the church here but later moved to the church at Wirksworth.

The Queens Counsel in the Market Place, Ilkeston, opened in 2007. It was previously a solicitor's office. It was winner of *The Ilkeston Advertiser* Best Bar in 2014.

The Paper Mill at Darley Abbey.

The Queen's Head, Ockbrook.

The Quiet Woman.

The Queen's Head at Ockbrook was once known as the Horse and Jockey. It changed its name to the Queen's Head on the accession of Queen Victoria in 1837. The Home Guard used the pub as its headquarters during World War Two.

The Quiet Woman at Earl Sterndale dates from the 16th century. The pub sign shows a headless woman, below which are the words 'Soft Words Turneth Away Wrath'. Its unusual name is based on the legend that the wife of a former landlord, known as Chattering Charteris, was such a nag that her husband eventually put an end to her rantings by cutting off her head. The approving villagers, who had also suffered her wrath, kept their mouths shut and had a collection to pay for a headstone. An alternative version of this story is that the landlord, returning from market one day, was met with a torrent of abuse from his angry wife. He stormed out of the house and declared that if he couldn't have a quiet woman inside the pub, he would have one outside and arranged to have the sign painted. Although unusual, the pub sign and the legend that goes with it is not unique. There are a handful of similar pub signs elsewhere in the country which go by the name of the Silent Woman or the Headless Woman.

The Royal Crown in Chaddesden, Derby, was previously known as the Royal Crown Derby and thus derived its name from the porcelain factory which was founded in Derby by William Duesbury in 1756. It became known as Royal Crown Derby in 1775 as a consequence of the patronage of King George III. Apart from the name, the pub has no connection with the porcelain manufactury.

The Saracen's Head, Shirley.

The Samuel Fox Country Inn at Bradwell takes its name from the famous inventor of the steel-framed umbrella. Born at Bradwell in 1815 Samuel Fox was the creator of the modern umbrella. In 1851 he and his company, Fox Umbrella Frames Ltd, developed the Paragon umbrella frame which was far superior to its competitors. He became a very rich man but continued to make regular visits to Bradwell. For many years he made anonymous donations to benefit the poor of the village.

The Saracen's Head at Shirley dates back to 1791 when it combined the functions of a farmhouse and hostelry, a not uncommon practice at the time. The Shirley family took their name from the village itself and an early member of the family died in 1190 at the Battle of Acre fighting against the Saracens. The family later adopted a Saracen's head as part of their crest. It is perhaps not surprising that this later became the name of the pub.

The Scotsman's Pack in Hathersage was originally known as the Scotchman's Pack. It takes its name from the packmen, as travelling drapers were sometimes known, who used to visit from Scotland in the 16th and 17th centuries with their wares of tweed and woollens. The inn also provided accommodation for the packhorse trains which regularly crossed the area with their loads of coal, wool, salt, corn and malt.

The Seven Wells at Etwall is a modern pub that takes its name from the wells in the village which for centuries supplied drinking water to the people who lived there. The name of the village is also significant, being derived from Etewelle meaning Eatta's

The Seven Wells at Etwall.

water or well. Since 1970 annual well dressing ceremonies have been held in the village. The Seven Wells is a Greene King Pub & Grill.

The Silk Mill pub in Derby takes its name from the nearby Silk Mill, which now houses Derby's industrial museum. A mural on the side of the pub depicts the events of the famous silk mill lockout of 1833-34. A dispute over a workman being fined for poor quality workmanship led to a strike by members of an early trade union. The employers retaliated by refusing to employ any man who was a member of a trade union and by hiring 'black-leg' labour. In the eyes of many this transformed the strike into a lock out. The strikers received support from

The Silk Mill, Derby.

many parts of the country, but fearing civil unrest the Mayor drafted in a number of special constables and a troop of dragoon guards. After a number of months, destitution and the fear of prosecution forced many men back to work. Those who were allowed to return to work were sometimes harshly treated, and in many cases found that their wages had been reduced. The Derby 'Lock Out' was one of the significant events in the history of the trade union movement. In April each year politicians and trade unionists meet to lay a wreath at the gates of the Silk Mill to commemorate the events of 1834.

The Silver Ghost in Alvaston, Derby, is a modern pub that takes its name from the iconic Silver Ghost motor car which was manufactured locally by Rolls-Royce in the first three decades of the 20th century. The Silver Ghost won many competitions and was popular with the aristocracy. It was bought by dukes, maharajas and even the Tsar of Russia. During World War One the Silver Ghost chassis was used in the building of ambulances and armoured cars. The famous Lawrence of Arabia used them to great effect in his guerrilla warfare against the Turks.

The Sir Barnes Wallis in Ripley is named after the famous engineer and inventor who was responsible for the bouncing bomb which was used on the famous 'Dambusters' raid on Germany in 1943. Born at Ripley in 1887, he was also responsible for the design of the Wellington bomber using the innovative geodetic method of construction. He later developed a number of deep penetration 'earthquake' bombs which were used to great effect against German strategic targets such as submarine pens and V2 rocket sites. After the war he worked for the British Aircraft Corporation on the design of hypersonic aircraft and swing-wing technology. He received a knighthood in 1968 but continued to be involved in a variety of projects until his death in 1979.

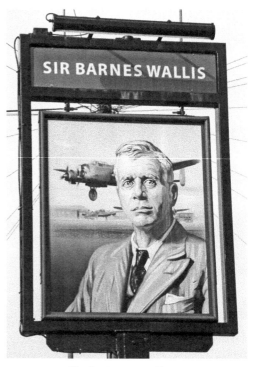

The Sir John Warren at Ilkeston is named after Sir John Borlaise Warren who was born at Stapleford just a few miles away across the border in Nottinghamshire. He joined the navy as an able seaman in 1771 but in 1774 he became Member of Parliament for Marlow and in 1775 was created a baronet. His naval career really began in 1777

The Sir Barnes Wallis sign.

The Sir Nigel Gresley, Swadlincote.

and only two years later he obtained his first command of a ship. In April 1794, in command of a squadron of frigates, he captured three French ships and in the years that followed he continued to effectively protect British seaborne trade. In 1796 he is said to have captured or destroyed over 200 enemy ships. His most significant achievement was probably the defeat, in 1798, of a French fleet carrying 5,000 men which was intended to land in Ireland. In 1802 he was appointed Ambassador Extraordinary to St Petersburg but he was soon back at sea and in 1806 he captured a large French ship, the *Marengo*. He became an admiral in 1810 and was commander-in-chief of the North American station in 1813-14. He died on 27 February 1822. A number of pubs in and around Nottingham are named after him.

The Sir Nigel Gresley is a modern pub in the centre of Swadlincote. Part of the Wetherspoons chain, it takes its name from the famous locomotive designer and engineer who, as a small boy, lived at nearby Netherseal where his father was rector of St Peter's Church. His interest in locomotives was stimulated by first seeing them on the Netherseal Colliery branch line. In later life he became Chief Mechanical Engineer of the London and North Easter Railway and was responsible for designing some of the most famous steam locomotives in Britain. His designs include the Flying Scotsman and the Mallard, which still holds the record for being the fastest steam locomotive in the world. He died in 1941 and is buried in Netherseal churchyard.

The Sitwell Arms at Morton near Alfreton takes is name from the Sitwell family of nearby Renishaw Hall. They were a distinguished family that contained several poets, writers and critics. Perhaps the most famous was Dame Edith Sitwell. She was the eldest of the three literary Sitwells, her brothers being Osbert and Sacheverell. Edith, who died in 1964, was an avant-garde poet and something of an upper-class eccentric who was renowned for her exotic clothing and over-sized jewellery.

The Soldier Dick pub at Furnace Vale is an 18th century coaching inn that lies on the main A6 Buxton to Stockport Road. According to legend, the pub name relates to a soldier who was given refuge here in the 17th century. He was wounded and was nursed back to health by the landlord's wife. It appears that he stayed on at the inn and became a popular local 'character' who could always be relied upon to entertain customers with tales of his adventures. He probably helped out as a pot man and may have been treated to drinks as a reward for regaling locals and visitors alike with his stirring tales.

The Stepping Stones at Ashbourne takes its name from the actual stepping stones over the River Dove at Dovedale. This is a popular feature which attracts thousands of visitors each year. In Victorian times you could hire a donkey from a character called 'Donkey Billy' to bring you to the Stepping Stones from Thorpe railway station. It is much easier to cross the river now because of the controversial refurbishment of the stones by Derbyshire County Council in 2010.

Smith's Tavern in Ashbourne takes its name from the family who owned it almost continuously from the 1850s until 1935. Its history can be traced back to 1851 when it was recorded as Smith's Wine Vaults, being owned by John Smith, a wine and spirit merchant. It is not clear when the business changed from being a wine and spirit merchant to a public house but it was certainly before 1946.

Smith's Tavern.

The Standing Order, Irongate, Derby.

The Standing Order in Irongate, Derby, opened in the mid-1990s in what was previously a branch of the National Westminster Bank. This Grade II listed building was originally built in the 1870s for Crompton and Evans Union Bank on the site of the old Talbot Inn. The Standing Order is part of the Wetherspoons chain and still houses oil paintings of a number of Derbyshire worthies.

The Stanhope Arms at Stanton-by-Dale takes its name from the Earls Stanhope who owned much of the land in the area and became Lords of the Manor in the 18th century. The 7th Earl Stanhope was commissioned as a second lieutenant in the Grenadier Guards and went with his battalion to serve in South Africa during the Second Boer War. In later life he went on to hold a number of government posts including President of the Board of Education, Leader of the House of Lords, First Lord of the Admiralty and Lord President of the Council. He sold the estate to the Stanton Ironworks Company in 1912.

The Strutt Arms at Milford, near Belper, is named after the local Strutt family who contributed a great deal to both Belper and Milford. Jedediah Strutt was a textile manufacturer and owner of cotton mills at Belper and elsewhere in Derbyshire. In 1758 he secured a patent for a machine to manufacture ribbed stockings. The 'Derby Rib' was a huge success and earned a fortune for Strutt, which he was able to use to develop a substantial hosiery business and provide the financial support for Arkwright's spinning mill at Cromford. The two men later went their separate ways and Strutt went on to develop mill communities at Belper and Milford. Strutt and his sons built houses, schools and chapels for their workers and established farms to provide cheap food and

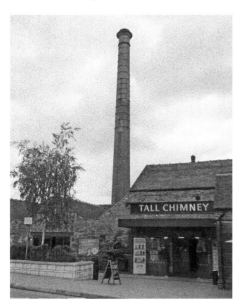

The Tall Chimney, Swadlincote.

milk. Other benefits included a sick club, a dancing room, an orchestra and a choir. The Strutts forbade corporal punishment and relied instead on a system of fines or forfeits to maintain good order and productivity in their mills. Jedediah Strutt died in 1797 and is buried in the Unitarian chapel he had built in Belper. There is also a Strutt Arms in Belper itself.

The Tall Chimney in Swadlincote opened in December 2011 in a renovated single-storey industrial building on a former pipeworks site (now a retail park). It takes its name from the nearby tall chimney which was part of Wragg's

*Plaque on the wall of the
Thomas Leaper pub.*

The Thomas Leaper, Derby.

Pipe Works. This company was responsible for the manufacture of sewage pipes which were supplied to local authorities throughout the country and across the world.

The Thomas Leaper in Irongate, Derby, is another Wetherspoons pub. The present building is the former Irongate House, an attractive four-storey building which was probably built in the 1740s. It stands on the site of the Leaper family residence. Not a great deal is known about the family, but in 1670 Thomas Leaper paid tax on nine hearths as required by the highly unpopular hearth tax levied on households at the time. In the 1880s the premises were acquired by the tailors Smith and Brigden and the firm (by 1891 known only at Brigdens) continued trading here until 1997. It was for many years a Yates Wine Lodge but later became part of the Wetherspoons group of pubs.

The Treble Bob in Barleston is a modern pub that opened in 1998. The name was derived from a bell ringing term which involves ringing a number of changes. This was rung at St James's Church in 1928 to commemorate the coming of age of Miss Stella Locker-Lampson, the daughter of Godfrey Locker Lampson MP, the last private owner of Barlborough Hall.

The Trent Lock public house at Sawley was previously known as the Navigation Inn. It takes its name from the Trent Lock which lies adjacent to the pub. As well as marking the point where the River Trent and River Soar meet with the Erewash Canal, the lock sits on the border of three counties: Leicestershire, Nottinghamshire and Derbyshire.

The Trent Lock pub.

The Walton Damnation is a micro-pub at Walton, a suburb of Chesterfield. It is tucked away in the far corner of the Walton Shopping complex. Previously a food take-away business, it opened in July 2017. Its name is a play on words. The Walton Dam is a small reservoir which has been used for a variety of leisure activities for over a century. Local people visit the area to fish, feed the ducks and just enjoy the countryside. Like a number of micro-pubs, the Walton Damnation serves four changing beers and is popular with lovers of real ale.

The Wanted Inn is a family-run country pub at Sparrowpit in the High Peak area of Derbyshire. The building is over 400 years old and was known for centuries as the Devonshire Arms. In 1956 it was offered for sale by auction but failed to attract a bidder. For almost two years it remained on the market, but no one wanted it. Finally, it was purchased, and on 27 October 1957 the then Minister of Works, the Rt. Hon. Hugh Molson MP, renamed it 'The Wanted Inn'. Today the pub styles itself as a 'Country Café and Bar'. In addition to providing food and drink, a shop also sells a wide range of snacks and gifts including home-made pork pies and Derbyshire oatcakes.

The Watts Russell Arms at Hopedale near Hartington takes its name from the 19th century industrialist who lived at nearby Ilam Hall. The son of an East End soap manufacturer, he was educated at Oxford University and married a wealthy heiress. He was Sheriff of Staffordshire from 1819 to 1820 and was described as 'one of those

Staffordshire landowners with no blood but immensely rich'. He was MP for the rotten borough of Gatton and later stood unsuccessfully for the parliamentary constituency of North Staffordshire. The diarist William Dyott noted that while 'not an orator' Watts Russell seemed, 'a worthy and most excellent man'. He owned estates in Staffordshire and Northamptonshire and used his wealth to rebuild Ilam Hall in the Gothic style.

The White Lion at Matlock used to be known as the Buddles Inn and this too reflects the lead mining heritage of the area. Buddle is the lead mining term meaning to wash lead ore in a trough. It is said that some such troughs used to stand directly outside the inn.

The Whitworth Arms Hotel in Darley Dale takes its name from Sir Joseph Whitworth, who made his home at nearby Stancliffe Hall in 1871, following his second marriage. By this time he had already achieved fame and fortune as the inventor of the British Standard screw system and the Whitworth rifle. He died in 1887 and was buried in the grounds of St Helen's Church, Darley Dale. Part of his bequest was used to construct the Whitworth Institute in the village.

The Wick in the Wardwick, Derby, was previously known as the Wardwick Tavern. It takes its name from the street in which it stands but also from Walber's Wick, the

The Wick, Derby.

Saxon farmstead that stood on this site over 1,000 years ago. The building itself has a long history. It was constructed in 1708 for the Alsopp family and later purchased by the Lowes, who built a brewery at the rear. This was substantially enlarged by the Alton family when they came into ownership in 1869. The brewery buildings were demolished in the 1930s to make way for a telephone exchange. Further changes in ownership ensued and for a number of years it was used as brewery offices. In 1969 Allied Breweries opened their redundant offices as a pub. At the time of writing the Wick was closed.

The Wilmot Arms at Chaddesden was originally known as the Wheel Inn but was renamed by the Wilmot family who lived at nearby Chaddesden Hall. Sir Henry Wilmot was a soldier. He served in the Crimea and India and was awarded the Victoria Cross in 1858. He went on to serve in China in the second Opium War. After leaving the army he was elected as Conservative Member of Parliament for South Derbyshire. The Wilmots remained at Chaddesden Hall until World War One but sold the estate in 1926. The hall was demolished a few years later. The Wilmot Arms dates from the early years of the nineteenth century. It is currently part of the Steamin' Billy chain of pubs.

The Windmill at Breadsall Hilltop is named after a tower mill that existed in the area from at least the start of the 19th century. It was demolished in the 1840s.

The Windmill Inn at Heage was previously known as the Green Man. It takes its name from the nearby Heage Windmill which was restored in 2002. This is a Grade II listed building and the only six-sailed stone tower windmill in the country. It is staffed by volunteers and is open to the public.

The Woodruff Arms in Hope was built on land originally owned by the Woodruff family. They played a large part in the life of the community over a period of several centuries. Members of the family fought at the Battle of Agincourt.

York Chambers was Long Eaton's first micro-pub and takes its name from the building in which it is located. Built in 1901-03, this Arts and Crafts building was designed by the architects Gorman and Ross and originally housed shops and offices. Many people fondly remember it as a café serving local residents for over 70 years.

The Young Vanish at Glapwell is named after a 19th-century champion racehorse. Originally the Blacksmith's Arms, the pub was renamed after a successful racehorse that won a number of races between 1827 and 1831. Vanish was stabled at nearby Glapwell Hall (since demolished). It is said that the pub got its name after a previous landlord won a considerable sum of money after placing a winning bet on the animal.

THE LAST DROP –
FACTOIDS AND ANECDOTES

Derby has been hailed by the Campaign for Real Ale as 'the real ale capital of the UK' and *The Lonely Planet Guide* describes Derby as 'the best place to drink real ale in the world'.

The Four Inns Walk is a challenge walk held annually over the high moorlands of the northern Peak District, mainly in Derbyshire. It is a competitive event without an overnight camp, involving teams of three or four walkers. It was first held in 1957 as a Rover Scout event but is now open to other teams of experienced hill walkers and fell runners. Originally the ruin of the Isle of Sky Inn was the starting point for a walk which took in the Snake Inn on the Snake Pass and the Nags Head at Edale. The finish was at the Cat and Fiddle above the Goyt Valley and, at 1,690ft, second only in height to Tann Hill in North Yorkshire as the highest pub in England. Disaster struck in 1964 when a sudden deterioration in the weather resulted in the tragic death of three competitors. The Four Inns Walk is widely regarded as the premier Scout-organised distance event in the country. It celebrated its Diamond Jubilee in 2017.

Revolution House, Chesterfield.

Revolution House on Whittington Moor near Chesterfield was once an ale house called the Cock and Pynot. It was here in 1688 that three conspirators met to plot the overthrow of King James II. The three conspirators were William Cavendish, Earl of Devonshire, the Earl of Danby and Mr John D'Arcy. A coded message was sent to William of Orange inviting him to seize the throne and plans were laid to raise armies in support of the invasion. In the event James II realised that his cause was hopeless and he was allowed to flee the country. William and his wife Mary were installed as joint monarchs.

One of the last legal cock fights in the county took place at the Bay Horse in Chesterfield in 1849. Legislation banning this pursuit was passed in the same year.

Statue of Michael Thomas Bass in Derby.

A government report, published in 1842, examined working conditions at the Stanton and Staveley Ironworks. For the men labouring in the forges, the work was hot and physically demanding and it is perhaps not surprising that the report found that they were more prone to drunkenness than colliers or other workers. In mitigation, however, it was stated that this was due to 'the very great thirst caused by their occupations'.

A statue of Michael Thomas Bass stands in Museum Square, Derby. A member of the famous brewing family, he was Liberal Member of Parliament for Derby from 1848 until 1883. He was a generous philanthropist and provided Derby with a library, a museum, a school of art, swimming baths and a recreation ground. He rejected the offer of a peerage and continued to serve in the House of Commons until shortly before his death in April 1884.

The 18th-century traveller John Byng (Viscount Torrington) stayed at various inns and taverns in Derbyshire. He always carried clean sheets in his baggage to reduce the ravages of inn lice.

In parts of Derbyshire, particularly in coal mining areas, some people still speak with a distinctive dialect. Derbyshire dialect words relating to food and drink include the following:

Beer-off	Off licence
Popping-up	Drunk (literally full of ale or 'pop')
Slotten	Drunk
Snap	Food

The Blue Peter, Derby.

Derby County football club won the FA Cup in 1946 and it was from the Blue Peter in Alvaston on 30 April 1946 that a brightly festooned Offiler's Brewery dray conveyed the victorious team to a civic reception at the Derby Council House.

The Derby Summer Beer festival has been held annually since 1977. The event now attracts thousands of people and showcases around 200 ales. In addition to the real ales on offer, visitors can also sample continental beers, ciders and perries as well as a choice of hot and cold food. Distinctive beer mugs are produced each year.

Chesterfield hosted the world's first ever gluten-free beer festival in February 2006.

A strange and terrifying tale is told of a doctor or medical student who, in the 18th century, was lodging at the Dolphin Inn at Derby. Having received what he believed to be a fresh corpse from a pair of grave robbers he set to work to dissect the body. Having opened the woman's stomach cavity

The Dolphin Inn, Derby.

The Newhaven House Hotel.

he found to his horror that she was still alive. Dragging herself from the table she ran screaming from the room, dragging her intestines behind her. Not surprisingly she did not survive this terrible ordeal. It is said that the unfortunate doctor was driven mad by this experience. According to some accounts the unfortunate woman continues to haunt the pub and her screams can sometimes be heard emanating from the cellars.

The Newhaven House Hotel, now closed, was once an important coaching inn on the Derby to Buxton turnpike. It was built by the Duke of Devonshire in 1705 and was named the Devonshire Arms. It was a large and well-proportioned building with stabling for 100 horses. According to legend, King George IV once stayed here on his royal travels. It is said that he was so impressed with the hospitality he received that he granted the inn a free and perpetual licence. At some point in the 19th century the inn became part of the Duke of Rutland's estate and may have been renamed at that time. At the time of writing the buildings appear to be undergoing some restoration.

Bakewell Pudding is a traditional dish which was first created in 1820 at the Rutland Arms in Bakewell. The cook was instructed to make a strawberry tart but for some reason she poured the mixture of eggs over the strawberry jam rather than mixing it into the pastry. The guests were enthusiastic in their praise of this new dish and it has been popular ever since. A number of shops in the town claim to hold the original recipe.

An urban myth from the first half of the 20th century concerns a group of men from Derby on a day trip to Blackpool. They came across a stranger in a pub rather the worse for wear and unable to tell them much about himself. On checking through his pockets, they discovered that like them he came from Derby. Keen to help a fellow Derbean, they put him on their coach and deposited him back at his mother's front door in Derby. She was surprised to see him as she thought he was on his honeymoon in Blackpool!

The house adjoining the church at Dale Abbey was once a pub – the Bluebell Inn. The whole building was originally the infirmary chapel of the abbey. It was probably unique in being attached to the only semi-detached church in the country. The pub has been a private house for many years but the church still holds services.

The Barrel Inn at Bretton stands at 1,200 feet above sea level and claims to be the highest pub in Derbyshire. In January 1947 the area experienced one of the most severe snow storms on record. With drifts as high as 20ft, the inn was entirely cut off for around a fortnight. When help finally arrived a tunnel had to be dug through to the front door to rescue the landlord, Stanley Drewitt, and his wife.

The Miners Standard at Winster was built in 1653. The date stone lies over the front door along with the initials EP; EP; FP. They stand for Edith, Ella and Frank Prince although according to locals they stand for, 'Every person, entering pays for a pint'.

The first written reference to a publican in Derbyshire concerns a certain William the Inn Keeper, who is mentioned in the records of Darley Abbey.

During the 19th century a number of rhymes were written which described the pubs in the village in an amusing manner. The following example is from Crich:

> As the Lord Nelson was staggering out of the Canal Inn,
> Watching the Red Lion devour the Shoulder of Mutton,
> He fell into the King's Arms who was standing under the Royal Oak
> Out of the Rising Sun, watching the Black Swan near the River of Time
> They both laughed when they saw the Jovial Dutchman
> Followed by the Greyhound who was taking The Wheatsheaf to
> The Bull which was grazing near The Cliff

A cast-iron plaque fixed to the Wardwick Tavern in Derby marks the level that the flood waters reached on 1 April 1842. This flood was caused when Markeaton Brook overflowed, causing much damage to the centre of the town.

The Green Man and Black's Head Royal Hotel at Ashbourne claimed for

Plaque commemorating the flood of 1842.

The Green Man and Black's Head pub sign.

many years to be the longest pub sign in the country. It came about when two inns, the Green Man and the Blackmoor's Head, were united in 1825. The addition of Royal came after Queen Victoria visited in the 1830s. Subsequently, the addition of 'Commercial' allowed the owner to claim it was the longest inn name in Britain. This claim is challenged today by 'The Old Cheshire Artillery Volunteer Rifleman Corps Inn' at Staleybridge in Tameside. The Green Man and Black's Head sign remains the longest in Derbyshire and still proudly straddles John Street in Ashbourne, to the delight of visitors and locals alike.

The Newton Wonder apple was first grown at the Hardinge Arms at Kings Newton. Samuel Taylor, the landlord, discovered a seedling in the roof gutter of his pub and planted it in the garden. It was from this tree that the first Newton Wonder apple was produced in 1870.

Until its closure in 2001 Dema Glass in Chesterfield produced large quantities of beer mugs for the pub trade. For many years they also produced the personalised half-pint glasses made for the Derby Beer Festivals.

Dick Turpin, the famous highwayman, is said to have visited some of the pubs in Derbyshire. The Holly Bush at Makeney, the White Hart at Bargate and the Peacock Inn at Oakerthorpe all lay claim to his patronage. Sadly, all this is the stuff of legend and there is no evidence that the infamous outlaw ever visited this part of the country.

The pub quiz originated in the mid-1970s. A recent survey estimated the number of pub quizzes held every week in Britain to be around 22,500. In Derbyshire it is possible to find a pub quiz somewhere on every day of the week, except Saturday. There is also a Derbyshire Pub Quiz League that organises a 'Brain of Derbyshire' competition each year.

The Derby Drinker is a magazine published by Derby CAMRA. In November 2018, with the support of the National lottery, it produced a special 'Armistice Edition' which described the impact of World War One on the pubs and breweries in Derby.

In 2013 the Angler's Rest at Bamford became the first community pub in Derbyshire when it was purchased collectively by over 300 people. Their plan was to create a community hub combining their pub with a café and post office. Today it is a flourishing enterprise supported by a dedicated group of volunteers. It recently featured in *The Guardian's* Top 50 pubs and in 2017 was named Sheffield CAMRA District Pub of the Year.

The colliers at Nadin's Colliery in South Derbyshire went on strike in 1842 following the withdrawal of the miners' free ale allowance.

The Tiger Inn, Turnditch, applied for a Guiness World record in 2016 for the highest number of pies it had on its menu. The bid was part of its contribution to British Pie Week when a total of 88 different pies were offered on the menu.

The Hardinge Arms at King's Newton.

The village of Hayfield featured in the TV series of *The Village*. The Royal Hotel became the fictional Lamb Inn but the actual pub interiors were filmed in the King's Arms Hotel in nearby Chapel en le Frith. The Royal Hotel did, however, benefit financially as several members of the cast and crew were accommodated there.

Some strange and unusual deaths have taken place in pubs. On 12 October 1881 *The Derby Mercury* reported the death of John Shaw, the landlord of the New Inn at Alfreton. Three weeks earlier he had been attempting to catch a wasp which was in the window of his house when he stumbled and cut his wrist on a broken pane of glass. He bled very much at the time and died from blood poisoning and the shock to his system. It was not deemed necessary to hold an inquest.

The Navigation Inn at Buxworth was at one time owned by Pat Phoenix who played the role of Elsie Tanner in the *Coronation Street* TV series from 1976 to 1984. She also starred in a short-lived sitcom, *Constant Hot Water*, in which she played a Bridlington landlady.

Daniel Defoe, who visited Derby in 1726, wrote that 'the trade of the town is chiefly in good malt and good ale; nor is the quantity of the latter unreasonably small, which as they say, they dispose of among themselves, though they spare some or their neighbours too'.

The Spotted Cow in Holbrook is owned by 225 people. Having closed its doors in 2014, campaigners from the Holbrook Community Society began a fight to buy

The Spotted Cow, Holbrook.

their beloved village pub. In 2016 it was declared an asset of community value and a total of 225 investors joined forces to buy the building and the adjacent car park. Following a period of restoration and renovation, it re-opened in July 2017. It now serves home-made food and a range of locally sourced beers from nearby micro-breweries. It has an unusual sign – a replica black and white cow!

The World Championship Hen Races are held in August each year at the Barley Mow in Bonsall. In addition to the races, prizes are also awarded in a wide range of categories including Best Turned Out Hen and Handler, Prettiest Hen and Most Well Travelled Hen. The pub is also home to the Chickenfoot Brewery.

The unusual pub sign at the Spotted Cow.

In 1684 the vicar of Eyam, the Reverend Hunt, got himself into trouble by getting married, whist he was drunk, to the daughter of the landlord of the Miners Arms. Although it was regarded by those present as a drunken prank and not a legal marriage, the Bishop got to hear of the matter. He insisted that the vicar marry the girl properly despite the fact that he was already engaged to another woman.

In September 1830 a seven-ton elephant named Mademoiselle d'Jaque stayed in the yard of the Green Man in Ashbourne while her master was accommodated at the inn. This amazing creature was on its way to Birmingham and meekly followed behind her master who rode on a pony.

A previous landlady of the Barley Mow at Kirk Ireton spent her entire life at the pub and had a reputation for maintaining tradition and resisting change. In 1971 she resisted decimalisation and up to until she died in 1976 she insisted that customers pay in 'old money'.

Chapel Street, Longnor, featured as the exterior of the Lamb Inn in the BBC TV mini-series of *Pride and Prejudice*

The Old Nag's Head at Edale dates from 1577. It marks the official start of the Pennine Way. This is a long-distance walk of 268 miles which goes from the Nag's Head through the Pennines, the Yorkshire Dales and Northumberland. It ends at the Border Hotel in Kirk Yetholm, just inside the Scottish border. The Nag's Head has been listed as one of the 100 greatest pubs in England and was visited by Julia Bradbury in the Peak District episode of her TV series *Best Walks with a View*.

Derby's first nightclub was the Balmoral Club in Charnwood Street. It was opened in 1963 by local entrepreneur Jack Holland. In addition to a restaurant and casino, the Stirling Room provided a stage for cabaret and an area for dancing to music provided by the Ken Barry Trio. A number of well-known entertainers appeared here including guitarist Bert Weedon, comedian Tommy Trinder and singer Elaine Delmar. It was a respectable and well-run establishment but that did not prevent some of the elderly and straight-laced ladies of the town giving it the nickname of the 'Immoral Club'!

The Old Moon Inn at Stoney Middleton was once the scene of a brutal murder. At some time in the middle of the 18th century a Scottish pedlar came to the Eyam Wakes to sell his wares. According to some accounts he reported another group of pedlars for trading without the appropriate licence. In their anger they murdered him in one of the outbuildings of the inn. The landlord is said to have turned a blind eye when they carted the body away to dump it in Carlswark Cavern in Middleton Dale. The body was discovered 20 years later and identified by the distinctive buckles on his shoes. The authenticity of this tale is borne out by an entry in Eyam parish register for 3 May 1773 when it was recorded that: 'Corpse and human bones found in a cavern in Eyam Dale by a person who was trying for a lead mine'.

Kings and queens feature in a number of Derbyshire pub names. The earliest mentioned monarch is King Alfred and the most recent is the King Edward VII, both at Alfreton. Other monarchs that have pubs named after them in Derbyshire include King William IV, Queen Victoria and several Georges. Even the Stuart pretender to the throne, Bonnie Prince Charlie, is commemorated at the Bonnie Prince at Chellaston near Derby. There is also a Prince of Wales in Ilkeston and a Princess Victoria in Matlock Bath. Pubs named after royalty that have since closed include the Prince Regent, the Queen Adelaide, the Royal Albert, the Prince Arthur and the King of Prussia. The British Queen, which stood in Brook Street, Derby, survived for only 30 years in the second half of the 19th century and was named after Queen Victoria.

The Horseshoe Inn at Longnor dates from 1609. It briefly achieved fame in an episode of the TV series *Peak Practice* under the pseudonym of the Black Swan.

In April 1758 two young runaway lovers, Alan and Clara, were making their way to Peak Forest (Derbyshire's Gretna Green). They stayed overnight at the Royal Oak Inn where they were noticed by a group of disreputable lead miners. The next day they waylaid the couple and robbed and murdered them. Their bodies were then thrown down a mine shaft. The remains were never discovered but their murderers all came to a sticky end.

The World Toe Wrestling Championships have been held in Derbyshire and Staffordshire for over 40 years. In recent years it has been hosted by the Bentley Brook Inn at Fenny Bentley near Ashbourne. Toe wrestling is similar to arm wrestling but using feet. Competitors lock toes over three bouts: right foot, then left foot and then right again. Before wrestling can begin, feet are carefully inspected by a professional podiatrist for any signs of fungal infection or injury.

Bess of Hardwick is a well-balanced hoppy bitter produced exclusively for the Hardwick Inn. The original Bess of Hardwick, the Countess of Shrewsbury, is probably best remembered for two things: surviving four husbands and building the nearby Hardwick Hall. She was a shrewd businesswoman and, apart from Queen Elizabeth I, was probably the most wealthy and powerful woman in the kingdom.

The Biker Guide lists a number of 'biker friendly' pubs in Derbyshire. These include the Hardinge Arms at Kings Newton, the Arkwright Arms at Chesterfield, the Fishpond at Matlock Bath and the Manifold Inn at Hartington.

For many years during the first part of the 20th century a penny farthing bicycle hung from one wall of the Bridge Inn at Derby.

In June 2010 a newborn baby boy was found abandoned at the Hawk and Buckle pub at Etwall. The baby, who was found in a bag, was taken to Derby Royal Hospital where he was named Jack by staff.

According to memories handed down over generations, bear baiting used to take place at the Shoulder of Mutton in Winster. Incredibly it is said that the bear slept in the back kitchen of the ale house in front of the fire!

The County and Station pub in Matlock Bath was, according to some accounts, originally two separate pubs, each catering for a different class of clientele. It is more likely that it was a single establishment with two separate rooms and possibly two entrances, each of which catered for a different class of customer. Whatever the truth of this story, it was certainly a single establishment by the 1890s. Its proximity to the railway station brought increased custom from visitors to the area. In June 1906 an inquest was held here into the death of a railway porter who had been knocked down by the Manchester to London Express while wheeling a barrow over the level crossing. The body was badly mangled, with the skull and some of the limbs torn away, so the task of the coroner's jury must have been difficult. At the time of writing the County and Station was closed.

Skittles has been a popular pub game for hundreds of years, although recently a number of pubs have converted their skittle alleys to restaurants or other uses. There are pub skittles leagues in several parts of the county including Ripley, Clay Cross, Alfreton and Belper.

The County and Station pub.

The Moulder's Arms in Riddings claims to be the only thatched pub in Derbyshire. It is known locally as the 'Thack'. Very much a community pub, it hosts dominoes, darts and skittles teams.

'Publican Murders Bailiff' was the headline in *The Derbyshire Times* in March 1907. The publican was Miles Gosling, landlord of the De Rodes Arms in Barlborough. The bailiff was William Mullinger, who was attempting to collect a debt of £60 on behalf of the brewery. After killing Mullinger, Miles Gosling went on to commit suicide.

Izaak Walton wrote in *The Complete Angler*: 'I will now lead you to an honest alehouse where we shall find a cleanly room, lavender in the windows, and twenty ballads stuck about the wall'.

During the early 1980s John O'Hare, the former Derby County and Nottingham Forest player, became landlord of the Scarsdale pub in Duffield following his retirement from professional football.

The Red Lion pub at the Tramway Village, Crich, originally stood outside the Tram Depot in Stoke on Trent. This was an original Victorian pub which for many years was patronised by the local tram workers. It was scheduled for demolition but following its closure in 1973 the facade was carefully taken down brick by brick by members of the Tramway Society. It remained stored in a field for a number of years and was eventually rebuilt as part of the recreated Victorian street scene at the museum. The pub's landlord at the time of demolition in the 1970s was Derek North and it was he who was chosen to

The Red Lion, Crich Tramway Village.

cut the tape at the official re-opening ceremony. The unsung hero of this enterprise was architect Jim Soper, a member of the society, who took thousands of bricks back to his home in West Yorkshire and methodically cleaned and repaired them in readiness for the reconstruction.

According to local legend, Dick Turpin, the infamous highwayman, is said to have once called at the remote Bull i' Thorn on the Buxton-Ashbourne Road. The pub itself is now sadly closed and neglected but there is no real evidence to support the legend. A more likely candidate is William Buxton. Born at Elton near Winster, for a brief period he preyed on travellers using this popular route. After robbing a stagecoach in 1780, he was pursued to Ashbourne where he was seized outside the Anchor Inn. He was tried, convicted and hanged at Derby only a short while later.

An egg-throwing contest used to be held on Easter Monday at the Chequers Inn, Ticknall. Although popular for over 50 years, it was stopped in 2003 on health and safety grounds

The Great Kinder Beer Barrel Challenge is an annual event where teams compete to carry a full nine-gallon barrel of beer over the trackless Kinder Moor from the Snake Pass Inn to the Old Nags Head at Edale. The origin of this event lies in a bet placed in 1998. The original challenge was laid down one January evening when local Edale shepherd Geoff Townsend complained to the landlord of the Old Nag's Head that they had run out of his favourite beer. He jokingly offered to collect a barrel of this beer from the Snake Pass Inn, only three miles away but over very difficult terrain. The landlord made a bargain that if Geoff succeeded he could have the barrel – and its contents. The thirsty shepherd soon recruited 12 friends to help carry the barrel on a borrowed mountain rescue stretcher. He won the bet and shared the beer with his helpers. The event is now held annually on a Saturday in mid-September. Only 11 teams may take part and competitors must construct their own barrel carrying device. Winners receive trophies, and of course a barrel of beer. Entertainment and refreshments are available at the inn throughout the afternoon and a great deal of money is raised for charity.

The Derby Mile is a famous pub crawl which has been a rite of passage and a favourite activity for stag and hen nights for several decades. The original route started at the Derbyshire Yeoman at Kingsway and continued along Ashbourne Road, ending at the Lord Nelson on the corner of Curzon Street and the Wardwick. The Derbyshire Yeoman closed in 1991 and was converted into a MacDonald's fast-food outlet. As a consequence, the Travellers Rest on Ashbourne Road became the new starting point. In its heyday 'milers' called at over a dozen pubs on their journey into the centre of the town. Many of these have now been closed but the Derby Mile remains a popular pub crawl with locals and students alike.

George Stephenson, the famous railway engineer, frequently stayed at the Wheatsheaf Inn at Crich whilst supervising the construction of links to the North Midland Railway.

The Black Swan at Idridgehay is said to have been used by George Elliott as the inspiration for 'The Wagon Overthrown' in her novel *Adam Bede*.

The Cross Keys Inn at Ockbrook was once the home of framework knitters. It is said that stockings for Queen Victoria and her court were made here. The long window under the eaves which provided light for the knitters is still visible.

The Navigation is a popular pub name. Almost all the pubs that share this name were built adjacent or close to a canal, often known as a 'navigation' in the 18th and 19th centuries. (The men who built these canals were known as navigators – shortened to navvies.) There are several pubs with this name in Derbyshire. Other pubs with links to the canals include the Canal Inn at Bullbridge, Trent Lock and the Lockkeepers Rest at Sawley and the Canal Turn at Spondon.

An interesting and amusing incident took place at the White Swan, Littleover, towards the end of World War Two. One night a soldier walked into the pub and said he was going to organise a raffle at one shilling a time for 12 pairs of ladies' stockings, a silver cigarette case and a string of beads, which he indicated were in the parcel he was carrying. Without seeking to see the contents of the parcel, people gave him money and after collecting more than £2 the soldier disappeared, leaving the parcel behind. The customers then opened it and found that it contained only brussels sprouts!

The soldier, Walter Edward Wood, a private in the RAOC, appeared at Derby Police Court in January 1945 charged with obtaining one shilling by false pretences. The case was dismissed under the Probation of Offenders Act after an Army Officer had told magistrates that Wood had applied to go overseas and that the decision would depend on the court proceedings. To add insult to injury, as far as the locals were concerned Police Superintendent Wilson told the magistrates that nobody in the White Swan had the 'gumption' to open the parcel before they gave him the money!

Towards the end of World War Two, Captain Stratton from Derby created a British country pub in the heart of the Rhur. He and his men took over what had previously been the German officer's barracks near Dusseldorf. Here beneath a swinging Dragon's Head sign, he and his comrades enjoyed a game of darts. This was accompanied by a few pints of Belgian beer and music provided by a German orchestra.

According to an account in *The Derbyshire Times and Chesterfield Herald* of 20 June 1903, 'just about fifty years ago a man known as Walking Jim footed from the Seven Stars, Derby to the White Swan, Belper Market Place (eight miles) and back covering the distance nine times or 72 miles in 12 hours without a rest except for a very little brandy and port at each of the pubs. About the same time another well-known gentleman, a Mr Whysall rode one of his horses from the Seven Stars, Derby to Belper Market Place in four minutes under half a hour'.

In 1577 the government conducted a census of the nation's alehouses and inns. It found about 20,000 distributed around the country. Derbyshire was credited with 726 alehouses and 18 inns. Derby alone had 61 in 1577 and by the 1690s as many as 120 of the 694 houses in the borough were licensed to sell ale!

BIBLIOGRAPHY

PRIMARY SOURCES

Newspapers

Derby Daily Telegraph

Derby Mercury

Derbyshire Advertiser and Journal

Derbyshire Courier

Derbyshire Times and Chesterfield Courier

Staffordshire Advertiser

Diaries, Journals, Guides etc

Black's Tourist Guide to Derbyshire, 1872

Defoe D. A Tour Through the Whole Island of Great Britain, 1724-6, London 1974

Feinnes C. (ed. C Morris), Journeys, London 1967

Moritz, C. P. (trans R Nettel), Journeys of a German in England – A Walking Tour of England in 1782, London 1983

The Torrington Diaries 1781-1794, (ed. C B Andrews), London 1971

Directories

Bulmer's Chesterfield and North- Eastern Derbyshire, 1895

Bulmer's Derby, 1895

Pigot and Co's Commercial Directory for Derbyshire, 1835

SECONDARY SOURCES

Allen J W, *Derby Coaching Days*, Derby 1977

Billson P, *Derby and the Midland Railway*, Derby 1996

Brown P, *The Pub*, London 2016

Brown P, *Man Walks into a Pub: A Sociable History of Beer*, London 2003

Brandwood G. et al, *Licensed to Sell* London, 2004

Craven M, *Inns & Taverns of Derby*, Derby 1992

Derbyshire Federation of Women's Institutes, *The Derbyshire Village Book*, Newbury, 1991

Dunkling L and Wright R, *The Wordsworth Dictionary of Pub Names*, London, 1987

Haydon P. *The English Pub: A History*, London 1994

Hey D, *Derbyshire: A History*, Lancaster 2008

Hopkinson F, *The Joy of Pubs*, London 2013

Jacks A, *The Old Dog and Duck: The Secret Meaning of Pub Names*, London 2009

Jennings P, *The Local: A History of the English Pub*, Stroud, 2010

Pentlow M. and Arkell P. *A Pub Crawl Through History*, London, 2010

Putman R. *Beers and Breweries of Britain,* Princess Risborough, 2004

Smith M. *A Derbyshire Miscellany*, Derby, 2013

Smith M. *Industrial Derbyshire*, Derby, 2008

Smith M. *Picture the Past – Chesterfield*, Derby

Thorburn G. *Pocket Guide to Pubs and Their Histories*, Barnsley, 2010

Turbutt G. *A History of Derbyshire (4 Vols),* Whitchurch, 1999

In conducting my research, I also made extensive use of a variety of magazines, journals, websites, individual village histories and museum displays. Conversations with local people also revealed some interesting and valuable information.

ND - #0316 - 270225 - C0 - 234/156/11 - PB - 9781780915890 - Gloss Lamination